With a unique ability to use wit and humor — and strong underlying commitment to scriptural authority, Ken Gaub seeks to focus on the questions facing the Church. This is a book every churchgoer should read.

— **Ron Stevens,** senior pastor,
Covina Assembly, Covina, California

Ken has the remarkable ability to clearly define sensitive issues without offense. This is his best work — and should have a healing effect on the Church.

— **Dale Carpenter,** senior pastor,
Stone Church, Yakima, Washington

Ken Gaub has been my friend for almost 20 years. His dynamic, humorous, and uplifting messages always have remarkable response. Ken is a true example of a Christian — always excited about the Lord.

— **Quentin Edwards,** International
Ministry, Dallas/Ft. Worth, Texas

Answers to Questions You've Always Wanted to Ask

Answers to Questions You've Always Wanted to Ask

by Ken Gaub

New Leaf Press

NEW LEAF PRESS EDITION
January 1994

Library of Congress Catalog Number: 91-61717
ISBN: 0-89221-207-1

Dedication

• To my wife, Barbara, who has stood with me through many years, and who spent hours typing the manuscript for this book.

• To my parents, John and Millie Gaub, whose prayers and support brought this ministry through many trials.

• To my brother Mike and my sisters Shirley, Carol, Esther, and Ruth, who know my faults and love me anyway.

• To my children, Nathan, Daniel, and Rebekah, and the members and the road crew of *Illustrator,* who have put reaching youth ahead of personal gain.

• To my office staff, board members, and personal friends, whose prayers and support help us reach a world for Christ.

• To Dan Wold, my closest friend of many years, who kept telling me to get the book done.

• Last of all, but not least, to Edna Bailey, without whose prayers, help, and encouragement this book still would not be finished.

Contents

*Is God a divine trickster, forever heaping
    trouble on unsuspecting man?*
How can I find the will of God for my life?
Why does a good God allow evil to exist?
*Amid all our troubles, how are we supposed to
    witness to unbelievers?*
How do you talk about God to total strangers?
How can you help your church grow?
What if nonbelievers want to argue?
*What if your life is such a mess that you are a
    lousy witness?*
*Is an enlightened, modern Christian really
    supposed to live up to old Victorian taboos
    about premarital or extramarital sex?*
*What's wrong with a Christian enjoying an
    occasional toke of marijuana or getting a
    little drunk?*
Is homosexuality forbidden in the Bible?
Is there a spiritual gift of judgment?

Isn't anybody here perfect? What is sin?
What happens if I do not forsake my sins?
What happens if God forgives me?
What do I have to do for God to forgive me?
Do I have to get baptized?
Does a Christian have to go to church?
Why does anybody go to church?

*What are we supposed to do about people who
    continue to sin?*
Are we servants or masters?

Foreword

Written in a unique style with humor and wit, this book is guaranteed to motivate Christians who want to make a difference in their generation, and make their lives count for God. The stories of personal happenings during Ken Gaub's worldwide ministry will continually remind the reader that serving God is exciting, challenging, and satisfying when one lives in the principles of success that God set forth in His Word. I recommend this book as a gift to friends who need to know that God has their number.

Dr. David Yonggi Cho
Seoul, Korea

Introduction

You can't believe everything you read . . . like many signs across America:

On a drive-thru restaurant:
- Pick up window,
- Drive through our window.

On a truck stop:
- Diesel/Fried Chicken.

At a road construction area:
- Flagman ahead, no shoulders.

At a shoe store:
- We sell only the right shoe.

In a photo store:
- For the holidays, let us blow up your kids.

You may or may not agree with everything in this book, but I do hope that it challenges you. I hope it helps you see that even in a mixed-up, troubled world you can have peace and be a success with God's help.

Bringing people to Christ is a lifestyle. It's the responsibility of every Christian to fulfill the

Great Commission, and that is not something you do only if your personality permits — you really have no choice!

Watching others bring people to Christ is not good enough. We are called to work in the Lord's vineyard. I know that many roads lead to hell, but no roads lead out.

The Need

According to the *World Almanac and Book of Facts,* there were less than 3 billion people on this planet in 1950. There are almost 5 billion now, and by the year 2000 there will be over 6 billion. Just one billion profess Christianity. More that 500 million are Muslim, and over 1.5 million of the Muslims are in America.

You are what you eat, drink, breathe, think, believe, and do. Your future depends on decisions and choices you make everyday.

If you keep doing what you do now, you will continue to get what you are getting now.

You can't go anywhere in life until you first decide exactly where it is you want to go. I know talent helps. However, today you are the result of many influences — parental, religious, educational, and social, plus whatever you have done with God's help to mold your own life.

You are meant to be an optimist, to develop, to dream, and to win others to Christ. God didn't make you because He was disappointed with monkeys. He has a plan for your life.

Ken Gaub

1

What Is the Proper Lifestyle for God's Rich and Righteous?

Are Christians promised immense wealth?

We live in a day when society in general and even many Christians place incredible importance on wealth. Many believe God wants us to be fabulously rich. Many teach that the wealth of the wicked is ours for the taking — that God is like a divine Robin Hood, taking from the dastardly and giving to the righteous. After all, the Old Testament is full of great, godly men whom God blessed. "Abram was very rich in cattle, in silver, and in gold," says Genesis 13:2.

King David "died in a good old age, full of days, riches, and honour," records 1 Chronicles 29:28.

"King Solomon exceeded all the kings of the earth for riches and for wisdom," proclaims 1 Kings 10:23.

God told Solomon, "Because this was in thine heart, and thou hast not asked riches, wealth, or honour, nor the life of thine enemies, neither yet hast asked long life; but hast asked wisdom and knowledge for thyself, that thou mayest judge my people, over whom I have made thee king: Wisdom and knowledge is granted unto thee; and I will give thee riches, and wealth, and honour, such as none of the kings have had that have been before thee, neither shall there any after thee have the like" (2 Chron. 1:11-12).

And so, today in many churches, prosperity is looked upon as a barometer of spirituality. Many Christians believe that the more financial assets we have, the closer to God we must be.

But is this teaching valid? Or can it go too far?

Some teachers did in the Early Church. A terrible extreme of this teaching is addressed in 1

Timothy 6:5. The apostle Paul was apparently concerned that young evangelist Timothy would be seduced into the highly persuasive, but twisted teaching of the day's Greed Gospel.

Paul strongly cautioned Timothy against Christians who consider Christianity to be a source of profit, a money-making business, and a good way to get rich. "From such withdraw!" Paul thundered — *Keep away from these people.*

Perhaps as a result, throughout history, Christianity has had a tradition of poverty, equating spirituality with being poor. Our forefathers were taught to respect barefoot mystics who swore vows of destitution — and lived as beggars, often in celibate seclusion, owning nothing.

But look what happened. While teaching and believing that poverty was God's way, the Church of history's dark Middle Ages was still immensely blessed. It accumulated marvelous treasures that today remain on display at the Vatican, throughout Europe, and in America's great museums.

Do you see the contradiction? Good people believed God did not have any interest in their gathering riches. They took oaths for life that they would possess nothing. But God blessed them anyway.

God's people continued to try to explain the paradox between the New Testament's cautions against loving money and the fact that through the Old Testament, God blessed His obedient servants with wealth.

One erroneous observation was that God's chosen people, the Jews, are often wealthy or at least blessed with an ability to manage their assets. So, the thinking was: When the Jewish leaders of first century Jerusalem rejected Jesus as the Messiah, their love of money became a sign to us of their depravity. Since we don't want to reject the Messiah, we must be the opposite: poor and ignoring good sense in managing the assets God gives us. Let's take a balanced view of this.

Was Jesus wealthy?

A very popular evangelist has a book out that proclaims Jesus was, indeed, very wealthy.

I agree. He owns the cattle on a thousand hills. At His command all that exists came into being. So, in terms of controlling or generating wealth, the man who was Jesus Christ was far wealthier than any earthly tycoon.

But it appears to me that while He was in human form He did not exercise any of His limitless options to manipulate earthly wealth for His own profit.

Did Jesus Christ, vagabond of Palestine, leader of fishermen and ex-tax collectors, have material wealth? Jesus is pictured as owning nothing, letting the devious Judas handle any money that came into His possession, having no house of His own, yet having all of God's creation at His single command.

Well, let's look at what the Bible has to say about this. When Satan tempted the Lord in the wilderness at the beginning of His ministry, Jesus certainly disdained any earthly riches or fame that Satan offered.

Satan, if you remember, took Him to a mountaintop and offered to give it all to Him.

Jesus declined in no uncertain terms.

The whole proposition was laughable, of course, and not just a little bit ironic. After all, Jesus was God on earth. He had created that mountain on which the two were standing and everything that Lucifer was displaying for Him to see.

Yet, as a man, He chose to own none of it — particularly if it was to be gained by Satan's influence.

What exactly, however, does the Bible say about Jesus being rich or poor? Well, here is a representative sampling:

> • Jesus replied, "Foxes have holes and birds of the air have nests, but the Son of Man has no place to lay his head" (Matt. 8:20;NIV).
> • They crucified him, and parted his garments, casting lots: that it might be fulfilled which was spoken by the prophet, They parted my garments among them, and upon my vesture did they cast lots (Matt. 27:35).
> • For ye know the grace of our Lord Jesus Christ, that, though

he was rich, yet for your sakes he
became poor, that ye through his
poverty might be rich (2 Cor. 8:9).

So, the question seems a bit obvious to me.
Jesus was rich as the Creator of all. Yet, as a man,
He elected to be poor.

Why? So He could be about His Father's
business — unencumbered by business concerns.

Must believers give away everything they own?

Look at Deuteronomy 8:18: "But remem-
ber the Lord your God, for it is he that gives you the
ability to produce wealth . . ." (NIV). That verse
tells me that we can pursue financial success, but
that we'd better remain gratefully mindful of our
Source, who loves us and wants the best for us.

"Praise the Lord," agrees Psalm 112:1-3.
"Blessed is the man who fears the Lord, who finds
great delight in his commands. His children will be
mighty in the land; the generation of the upright
will be blessed. Wealth and riches are in his house
. . ." (NIV).

Try out this long promise, direct from God
your Father:

My son, forget not my law;
but let thine heart keep my commandments: For length of days, and
long life, and peace, shall they add to
thee.

Trust in the Lord with all thine heart; and lean not unto thine own understanding. In all thy ways acknowledge him, and he shall direct thy paths. Be not wise in thine own eyes: fear the Lord, and depart from evil.

Honour the Lord with thy substance, and with the firstfruits of all thine increase: So shall thy barns be filled with plenty, and thy presses shall burst out with new wine. My son, despise not the chastening of the Lord: neither be weary of his correction: For whom the Lord loveth he correcteth; even as a father the son in whom he delighteth. Happy is the one that findeth wisdom, and the man that getteth understanding. For the merchandise of it is better than the merchandise of silver, and the gain thereof than fine gold. She is more precious than rubies: and all the things thou canst desire are not to be compared unto her (Prov. 3:9-15).

That passage tells me God blesses us with prosperity — but is very disappointed in us if we forget that so many things are more important than mere physical wealth.

"Riches and honour are with me; yea, durable riches and righteousness," proclaims Proverbs 8:18, but keep reading: "By humility and the fear of the Lord are riches, and honour, and life," adds Proverbs 22:4.

You've heard this one quoted: "Give, and it shall be given unto you; good measure, pressed down, and shaken together, and running over . . . . For with the same measure that ye mete withal it shall be measured to you again" (Luke 6:38). Be cautious of preachers who only quote that one when it's time to pass the plate. The verse is about generosity — and not just giving to clergymen.

"My God shall supply all your need according to his riches in glory by Christ Jesus" (Phil. 4:19).

What a great God we have!

2

Who Are "Uninformed Experts"?

**How can we tell who
knows what they're
talking about?**

It has always bothered me when someone
tells me that something can't be done. It really irks
me when they interrupt me with this insight while
I am doing it.

This world has always had, has now, and
always will have, uninformed experts. They read

all the books, know all the theories, but have no practical experience. Others don't know how to work with people, keeping their attitude straight and their mouth shut. Many times there is trouble or turmoil when they are present.

It's a wonder how some who have had no experience in a certain field have all the answers. In such things as matters of health, finance, and other really important things, it's always best to seek the advice of a true professional.

An uninformed expert usually knows everything, especially the negative aspects of any situation. Their pessimism breeds discouragement, lack of confidence, and gloom. They are quick to blame others for their problems, and usually can't see their own faults. Many of them seem to enjoy being miserable, and are happiest when they have made everyone else as miserable as they are.

They often feel a real need to control and are so insecure they can't admit to not knowing everything. No matter what the situation is they have been there or used to do that. They think management is wrong, (unless they are management) and only they in the whole world are right. How sad for them.

Years ago, I decided to buy a new, 40-foot Silver Eagle Coach — the type used by Continental Trailways then — for our musical family to travel in. People first told me there was no way I would be able to afford it. It took some time, and some doing, but when I finally could get the coach, they said it was a fluke, that it shouldn't have happened.

Then some of them tried to tell me how to maintain it. An older mechanic told me to warm up the engine for 30 minutes before taking off, and not to shut it down for stops of less than 30 minutes, but to let it run on "high idle." Other well-meaning friends told me I was wasting fuel.

He told me if I would wind it up on the hills, and not to lug down the engine, that it would last a lot longer and save money.

I decided to listen to the professional mechanic — not the uninformed experts, some of whom were friends and meant well.

The mechanic gave me solid advice, straight from the manufacturer's manuals. The result was that we drove that coach for more than 12 years, putting on over 600,000 trouble-free miles.

Maybe my friends were experts in some things, but as far as the care of a diesel engine was concerned, they were uninformed.

We've been taking tours to Israel for over half our lives. Through trial and error in earlier years we learned how to conduct a deluxe tour with no gimmicks, without cutting corners, and with no extra charges along the way. We know you can go cheaper, and most of the reasons why. Basically, you usually get what you pay for.

We have helped many pastors put tours together, and those who listen to our voice of experience do a great job. Others ignore what we say and have to learn by experience such things as avoiding certain budget hotels, trying to cross into certain countries without visas, or that it may cost

extra to continue to sites that you're really interested in visiting. These are just a few of the pitfalls.

If you really want your life to count for God,
learn from those who are doing it and not just
talking about it. Paul was able to say, "Those
things, which ye have both learned, and received,
and heard, and seen in me, do . . ." (Phil. 4:9).

Most of us are experts in something. We
may not even be aware that we are. However, we
can learn much from each other.

I love God, but my love for Him is more
than a feeling. It is a commitment. We need to be
aware of our mission in life and not get confused by
outside influences.

If you want God to work His plan in your
life, you need the help of God, who is the true
motivator. God will turn you on, light your fire, flip
your switch, ring your bell, and you can become a
master soul winner, and a success in life. Of
course, success means different things to different
people, but the same principles apply for getting
there.

Let's talk about being motivated for success.

How can we become "motivated for success?"

There are two types of motivation: internal
and external. Both are needed. The external comes
from speakers, books, tapes, and videos. The internal one comes from God-given dreams and goals

— and the desire to touch lives.

Look around you at the people who are working for God, and watch how they do it. I don't necessarily mean just those who are in the pulpit, but at the saints you sit with each Sunday. In almost every congregation you will see those whose lives really count, even though they may be quiet and unassuming.

Watch them (not to be looking for flaws), see what they do, and maybe learn to adapt some of their methods to your own personality. Maybe a little something they do will help you adapt to doing something better.

No one can give you an exact formula for being used of God, because no two people on this earth are exactly alike, and no two situations are exactly alike. Bloom where you are planted.

My wife, Barb, and I are very different, and that is putting it very mildly. To begin with, she is a woman, and she says women tend to think with their emotions, not always with their minds. I am right-handed, she is left-handed. I am an extrovert, she is calm and quiet. I am somewhat impulsive, she is slow and deliberate. I tend to be fussy about what I eat, she will try nearly anything once. I won't elaborate further, but you see what I mean.

She has told me that if she were to use my methods of witnessing and blessing people, she would feel like a fool. But she is willing to ask God to help her and use her. Her life does have an impact for the Master, and she has won people to Christ.

While she is more reticent about talking to strangers, when an opportunity does present itself, she is not hesitant about speaking out about the things of God.

I have seen her testify of the power of God in her life to heal to people who were scoffing at the thought of God healing today. Read my book, *God's Got Your Number* (New Leaf Press, Green Forest, AR) for the story of her healing of cancer.

Don't get discouraged, panic, or give up. Failure is the closest thing to success. (They say love is the closest thing to hate.) Be willing to take a chance. Go out of your way. Do something you have never done to reach out and touch someone hurting.

God wants to use you. You may never teach a class, sing in the choir, or serve on the board. But by witnessing you can be one of the most important soldiers in God's army.

Raise the quality of your thinking. Learn to be creative in your witness. Look for a need and fill it. The list is endless. You can make it work; you are in partnership with God. There are people all around you who hurt and who need the love of God. Let your life be the pipe that the water of His love can flow through to a needy and thirsty world.

You have unique traits and opportunities. God wants to use you. You don't have to be an uninformed expert. Get informed; become an expert soul winner. Reach out and touch someone today for Christ. Help heal a hurt. Help lift a burden.

What happens to a Christian who gets greedy and ungrateful?

"Danger! Danger!" are the words of Robbie the Robot of that old TV show "Lost in Space." The person who is blessed of God and does not remember his Source is in real danger.

> . . . bless the Lord thy God for the good land which he hath given thee. Beware that thou forget not the Lord thy God . . . when thou has eaten and art full, and hast built goodly houses, and dwelt therein; And when thy herds and thy flocks multiply, and thy silver and thy gold is multiplied, and all that thou hast is multiplied; Then thine heart be lifted up, and thou forget the Lord thy God . . . .
> But thou shalt remember the Lord thy God: for it is he that giveth thee power to get wealth . . . (Deut. 8:10-14, 18).

"He that trusteth in his riches shall fall: but the righteous shall flourish as a branch" cautions Proverbs 11:28.

"Labour not to be rich," warns Proverbs 23:4-5, "cease from thine own wisdom . . . riches certainly make themselves wings; they fly away as an eagle toward heaven."

And there's always this familiar verse:

> For the love of money is the root of all evil: which while some coveted after it, they have erred from the faith, and pierced themselves through with many sorrows.
>
> Charge them that are rich in this world, that they be not highminded, nor trust in uncertain riches, but in the living God, who giveth us richly all things to enjoy; That they do good, that they be rich in good works, ready to distribute, willing to communicate; Laying up in store for themselves a good foundation against the time to come, that you may lay hold on eternal life (1 Tim. 6:10, 17-19).

Will God take riches away from the unworthy?

Absolutely. Read some of those warnings again, then consider these commandments of God, stated in Deuteronomy 28:14-28 (NIV) in no uncertain terms:

> If you do not obey the Lord your God . . . all these curses will come upon you and overtake you:

- You will be cursed in the city and
  - cursed in the country.
  - Your basket and your kneading will be cursed.
  - The fruit of your womb will be cursed, and
  - the crops of your land, and the calves of your herds and the lambs of your flocks.
  - You will be cursed when you come in and
  - cursed when you go out.
  - The Lord will send on you curses, confusion and rebuke in everything you put your hand to,
  - until you are destroyed and come to sudden ruin because of the evil you have done in forsaking him.
  - The Lord will plague you with diseases until he has destroyed you from the land you are entering to possess.
  - The Lord will strike you with wasting disease, with fever and inflammation, with scorching heat and drought, with blight and mildew, which will plague you until you perish.
  - The sky over your head will be bronze, the ground beneath you iron.

• The Lord will turn the rain of your country into dust and powder; it will come down from the skies until you are destroyed.

• The Lord will cause you to be defeated before your enemies.

• You will come at that from one direction but flee from them in seven, and you will become a thing of horror to all the kingdoms on earth.

• Your carcass will be food for all the birds of the air and the beasts of the earth, and there will be no one to frighten them away.

• The Lord will afflict you with the boils of Egypt and with tumors, festering sores and the itch, from which you cannot be cured.

• The Lord will afflict you with madness, blindness and confusion of mind.

First Timothy 6:17-19 repeats similar but less drastic condemnation to the ungrateful.

So, how are you and I supposed to live — shunning wealth or pursuing it?

Let's take a balanced look at this.

God's Word teaches us that it is God's will for His obedient servants to be blessed not only physically, emotionally, and spiritually, but also financially.

Third John 2 says, "Beloved, I wish above all things that thou mayest prosper and be in health, even as thy soul prospereth." God is a giver, and we should follow His example. Luke 6:38 tells us to "Give, and it shall be given unto you." His Word teaches that He wants us to experience blessings. Being blessed in any way glorifies God.

But we cannot say poverty is a sign of spiritual failure any more than we can say wealth is an indicator of righteousness.

I've been in most of the poverty-stricken countries of the world. If you go there the terrible conditions in which the destitute live will tear at your heart. Does God want them to starve?

No. Satan has hijacked their inheritance. The gospel message raises the standard of living in the nations where it is strongly preached.

We need a right attitude about financial blessing. Jim Agard, a friend of mine, says that it's okay to own possessions. Just don't let possessions own you.

We also have to be careful that we don't lead unbelievers to think Christianity is a get-rich-quick scheme.

We Christians don't really own anything. All that we have is a gift from God which we must immediately present back to Him — and listen for His still, small voice guiding us as to what we're to do with His gift. We are just caretakers or stewards. It all belongs to God. Luke 12:15 tells you that "a man's life consisteth not in the abundance of things which he possesseth." Second Corinthians 6:10 says, ". . . having nothing, yet possessing all things."

Money and material things are neither good nor bad. They can be used for God or Satan. Don't forget Matthew 6:21 says, "For where your treasure is, there will your heart be also." The most important thing is your attitude. Your motives. Why you do what you do.

Let's take a look at what Jesus said in Matthew 6:33. "But seek ye first the kingdom of God, and his righteousness; and all these things shall be added unto you."

Jesus spoke not to a few chosen disciples, but to a multitude seated on a hillside in the beautiful countryside of Galilee.

He had admonished them that since God cares for the flowers surrounding them and the birds that were flying around, they need not be too concerned about their needs, but should see to putting God first.

His promise was, and still is, that God would see that they lacked for nothing. Seeking God and His righteousness had to be a priority in their lives, and should be in ours, also.

What is the righteousness that He speaks about? He had told them earlier that unless their lives were better than those of the Pharisees, they wouldn't make it into heaven.

Chapters 5 through 7 of the Gospel of Matthew contain some very stern warnings, but they also contain excellent rules of conduct and rich promises.

Elsewhere, Jesus repeated the commandment given in Deuteronomy 6:5, "And thou shalt love the Lord thy God with all thine heart, and with all thy soul, and with all thy might," adding, "and thou shalt love thy neighbor as thyself" (Matt. 19:19).

3

Are My Nice non-Christian Friends Really Going to Hell?

How can we qualify for God's blessings?

> We can't.
>
> On our own, by ourselves, without help, it is

not possible to fulfill the demands of our holy and just God.

Oh, dear! What do we do, then?

God's law says that when we disobey His rules of conduct, we must be punished.

Oh, dear! If we put ourselves in the hands of justice, we would be doomed to terrible vengeance.

However, in the Old Testament, our loving Lord accepted sacrifices to make up for His people's sins. He allowed His people to atone for their sins by sacrificing their possessions, principally livestock back then. From time to time they had to kill their finest cattle and burn it on an altar as a gift to their Creator, making up for their evil deeds.

Basically, you might say that they paid periodic fines for all the wrong they had done since their last burned sacrifice.

Well, God then made it easier for us. He allowed His own Son to come live among us for 33 years, back during the time of the Roman Empire.

God's people rejected Jesus and He was murdered after a sham trial. He was executed like a common criminal, killed on a dark afternoon at the same time that two thieves paid the ultimate penalty for their sins.

But Jesus had no sins. Instead, He was dying as a sacrifice for your and my sins — so that we wouldn't have to burn sacrifices of livestock ever again.

Are we completely off
the hook for our sins?

No! We have to accept the gift.

We must make peace with God. Then, as we seek god and His will for our lives, we miraculously begin to receive His blessings.

When we ask Him for help, He responds. But if our lives are not holy, if we are harboring bad feelings, if we have not forgiven, if we keep bringing up past hurts or wrongs, then He withholds all that He would give to us.

On our own, we can make some things happen, but not what could happen if you allowed God to have full control of your life.

Do we still have to obey
God's commandments?

There is a Bible concept that we need to look at very carefully. In John 14:15 Christ said, "If you love me, keep my commandments." This gives us a way to prove our love. One of His last commandments was, "Go ye into all the world, and preach the gospel to every creature" (Mark 16:15). If we love Christ, then the proof of this will be in our lives.

This call is separate from the call of the evangelist. This is the call for every one who follows Christ because of the richness of what He has done in our lives, to share Christ with others.

Many church members have it all backwards. They pay to bring in an evangelist, pay to advertise his crusade, and hope that a large crowd of sinners will be attracted and get saved.

These church members then sit on padded pews in a beautiful, air-conditioned building singing "Standing on the Promises," when they are really merely sitting on the premises. They don't want to do anything which inconveniences them. The money they put in the plate to pay for the visiting evangelist is not anything close to a sacrifice.

It's not wrong to bring in evangelists to win souls, but that is only part of what the Lord requires.

Your pastor should not be expected to be the prime soul winner in any congregation. Everybody should be winning souls. The pastor's main task should be teaching, thus leading the flock to maturity. Will we ever learn? Quentin Edwards, a friend of mine and a great preacher, said if a mule kicks you a second time you have a major problem.

We should be filled with a gnawing sense of responsibility.

Is there more than one God?

"The Lord he is God; there is none else beside him," says Deuteronomy 4:35. "Ye shall not go after other gods, of the gods of the people which are round about you," warns Deuteronomy 6:14.

Does that mean that there are other gods?

"I am the Lord, and there is none else, there

is no God beside me . . . from the rising of the and from the west, there is none beside me" (Isa. 45:5-6).

But there are *false* gods. Bogus dudes from Hades. Evil entities from hell that throughout history have masqueraded as magical, mystical beings, deceiving mankind for the obvious purpose of diverting you and me from the One true way to heaven. Second Corinthians 4:4 tells about "the god of this world" who has "blinded the minds of them which believe not."

Jesus Christ is the only way to God. "For there is one God, and one mediator between God and men, the man Christ Jesus" (1 Tim. 2:5).

While that may seem somewhat closed-minded of God, our Creator is very explicit about the way that He wants things done: "Neither is there salvation in any other: for there is none other name under heaven given among men, whereby we must be saved" (Acts 4:12).

"I am the door: by me if any man enter in, he shall be saved, and shall go in and out, and find pasture . . . . I and my Father are one," proclaims Jesus in John 10:9, 30.

In John 14:6, Christ proclaims again: "I am the way, the truth, and the life: no man cometh unto the Father, but by me."

Will God accept us if we simply live a good and moral life?

You and I have heard the argument so many

times: A great and loving God is not going to punish good people.

It makes good sense. Unfortunately, none of us can be good enough.

We all sin. We all blow it constantly. *Even me.* Or perhaps I should say, "Especially me."

Fortunately, my loving God has put together a way for me to be able to get into heaven anyway. He sent His Son to earth to be punished for all the terrible things I ever did. And all the rotten things you ever did.

And since Jesus took the punishment — including a particularly nasty, public death sentence — the price has been paid.

But aren't some people so saintly that they'll get into heaven anyway? I mean, what about such seemingly righteous non-Christians as Gandhi? Or Anwar Sadat or Confucius or Albert Einstein?

Compared with the goodness of God, "all our righteousness is as filthy rags," proclaimed the great, holy prophet Isaiah.

"The curse is poured upon us because we have sinned against you," lamented one of the most godly men who ever lived, the prophet Daniel.

"For all have sinned, and come short of the glory of God" (Rom. 3:23).

So, what can we do to get into heaven?

"He that *believeth* and is *baptized* shall be saved; but he that believeth not shall be damned," says Mark 16:16.

"For God so loved the world, that he gave his only begotten Son, that whosoever *believeth* in him should not perish, but have everlasting life," promises John 3:16.

That's pretty simple, wouldn't you say?

Well, there's more. Keep reading.

Why does God have us in the world?

"What is man, that thou art mindful of him? . . . For thou hast made him a little lower than the angels, and hast crowned him with glory and honour," mused David in Psalm 8:4-5.

I believe the answer for why God puts up with us and all our problems is basically that He likes us. He'd have to.

Actually, more than that, He loves us.

"Then God said, 'Let us make man in my image, after our likeness . . . .' God blessed them and said to them, 'Be fruitful and increase in number; fill the earth and subdue it . . .' " (Gen. 1:26, 28;NIV).

To demonstrate His love for us, He sometimes allows us to accumulate some degree of prosperity — if we are being obedient to Him in other things.

So, are we here to have a good time? Or are we to live somber, sober lives of meditation and penitence? Yes. Both.

We are supposed to have a great time in the joy of a wondrous God who demands our gratitude, obedience, and reverence.

What about the ungrateful, disobedient, and irreverent who are happy and wealthy? Well, Satan also rewards those who rebel and do his bidding.

You don't have to be a sex-obsessed Satanist dabbling in human sacrifice to receive the devil's evil blessings. He rewards those who ignore what God wants out of us.

But the trade-off is so terrible!

By giving in to the devil, you get wealth here on earth as well as the immense misery with which he delights in tormenting his people. Their wealth is never enough!

But by following our Father, we receive marvelous blessings, as well as contentment with what He has blessed us. We live in peace. When we die, we reign with the Lord forever.

Satan's followers get to stay with him for eternity, too. There they find that his torment on earth was only a brief taste of what awaits them for all time.

So, why does God put us in the world?

" '. . . I will dwell in them, and walk in them; and I will be their God, and they shall be my people. . . . And will be a Father unto you, and ye shall be my sons and daughters,' saith the Lord Almighty" (2 Cor. 6:16,18).

"But ye are a chosen generation, a royal priesthood, an holy nation, a peculiar people; that ye should show forth the praises of him who hath called you out of darkness into his marvelous light" (1 Pet. 2:9).

". . . for thy pleasure they are and were created" (Rev. 4:11).

Is God a divine trickster, forever heaping trouble on unsuspecting man?

Some people actually believe that He is out to torment us. Where do you think we get such obnoxious terms as "acts of God" in insurance policies?

To the contrary, lousy things are not acts of God. He is good.

He protects us from the rotten acts of Satan — which the devil loves to blame on the Creator.

"The beloved of the Lord shall dwell in safety by him; and the Lord shall cover him all the day long . . . . The eternal God is thy refuge, and underneath are the everlasting arms: and he shall thrust out the enemy from before thee" promises Deuteronomy 33:12,27.

"With long life will I satisfy him, and show him my salvation" (Ps. 91:16).

Marveling at the wonderful creation that God had made, David wrote, "I will praise thee: for I am fearfully and wonderfully made: marvelous are thy works . . ." (Ps. 139:14).

"If ye then, being evil, know how to give good gifts unto your children, how much more shall your Father which is in heaven give good things to them that ask him?" (Matt. 7:11).

"Are not two sparrows sold for a penny? Yet

not one of them will fall to the ground apart from the will of your Father. And even the very hairs of your head are all numbered. So don't be afraid; you are worth more than many sparrows," promises Matthew 10:29-31;NIV.

I really believe we are born to touch the lives of others. God has a plan for your life. We were born for a reason. You might say, "What is God's plan for me? I don't have any talent."

How can I find the will of God for my life?

"Wait on the Lord: be of good courage, and he shall strengthen thine heart: wait, I say, on the Lord," counsels Psalm 27:14.

"I will instruct thee and teach thee in the way which thou shalt go. I will guide thee with mine eye," promises Psalm 32:8.

"In all thy ways acknowledge him, and he shall direct thy paths," add Proverbs 3:6.

The prophet Hosea preached, "Come, and let us return unto the Lord: for he hath torn, and he will heal us; he hath smitten, and he will bind us up. After two days he will revive us . . . he will raise us up . . ." (Hos. 6:1-2).

"Ask, and it shall be given you; seek, and ye shall find; knock, and it shall be opened unto you: For every one that asketh findeth; and he that seeketh findeth; and to him that knocketh it shall be opened," assures Matthew 7:7-8.

Well, I could go on and on, quoting the wonderful promises that fill the Bible. My point is that God is not out to get us.

He loves us. His promises are full of all sorts of incredible assurances such as: "the Spirit of truth, is come, he will guide you into all truth . . ." (John 16:13).

"If any of you lack wisdom, let him ask of God, that giveth to all men liberally . . . and it shall be given him. But let him ask in faith, nothing wavering . . ." (James 1:5-6).

"Draw nigh to God, and he will draw nigh to you," proclaims James 4:8.

Why does a good God allow evil to exist?

Did your parents ever spank you?

Did they ever make you stand in the corner?

I have a friend whose wife was having a terrible time with her fourth-grader, a strong-willed daughter with a sharp wit and a quick mouth.

She sought help from a Christian counselor who talked about demonstrating her love to the child by being warm and affectionate . . . as well as stern and firm.

"The next time the little darling starts scream- ing and accusing you," this Christian counselor told the mother, "throw a glass of cold water on her. Shock her. Stop her. Then correct her in love."

While dousing the kid seemed a bit drastic, it was incredibly effective. The next time that the nine-year-old went into a tirade, this Christian mom calmly picked up a glass of ice water and tossed it in the child's face.

"Mommmmmmmmy!" sputtered the pre-teen.

"Be quiet and listen to me," said the mother. "Now listen: You are going to mind me because I am the mother, that's why. You're not the mother. I am. Now, go do what I said."

Meekly, the child did.

Often that's what God does to you and me.

God has "set before you life and death, blessing and cursing: therefore choose life, that both thou and thy seed may live: That thou mayest love the Lord thy God, and that thou mayest obey his voice . . . for he is thy life, and the length of thy days," explains Deuteronomy 30:19-20.

"Choose you this day whom ye will serve . . . as for me and my house, we will serve the Lord," proclaimed Joshua in Joshua 24:15, whom God blessed incredibly — allowing this great general to defeat vast armies that resisted God's people as they returned from Egypt to resettle the Promised Land.

But Joshua was not completely obedient. He didn't kick out all the pagans that God ordered be removed from Israeli territory. The result is still giving Israel difficulty today, for God told him, "I also will not henceforth drive out any from before them of the nations which Joshua left when he died: That through them I may prove Israel, whether they will keep the way of the Lord to walk therein, as their fathers did keep it, or not" (Judg. 2:21-22).

What does that mean? God let the Philistines stick around to give Israel a bad time every so often so that the Israelis didn't forget who was their protector and provider.

When they called on Him, He made the Philistines behave. But when the Israelis didn't ask for help, they didn't get any. God just let them fight their own battles.

And they lost quite a number of times.

Today, the Philistines are still in Israel. In modern English, they are called "Palestinians." But in most of the other languages of the earth, such as Spanish, they still go by their historical name. Yasir Arafat is a direct descendant and cultural heir of the same guys who cut Samson's hair.

God uses jerks to keep us in line.

"Fret not thyself because of evil men, neither be envious at the wicked; for there shall be no reward to the evil man; the candle of the wicked shall be put out," warns Proverbs 24:19-20.

"We give glory in tribulations also," wrote Paul in Romans 5:3-4, "knowing that tribulation worketh patience; And patience, experience; and experience, hope."

"For our light affliction, which is but for a moment, worketh for us a far more exceeding and eternal weight of glory" (2 Cor. 4:17).

You need to understand that you are in a war. Satan loves trying to defeat you. If you attempt to fight back without God's help, the devil will knock you to your knees.

You can help tip the scales of the battle in your favor by your obedience to the Word of God or you can lose the battle by your disobedience, stubbornness, and unforgiving spirit. Deuteronomy 28 discusses this quite thoroughly. We often help create our own problems, but we can also overcome them with God's help.

Amid all our troubles, how are we supposed to witness to unbelievers?

As Jesus left this earth to return to His Father, He said, "You shall be witnesses unto me." A witness is not something that you choose to be. If you see an automobile accident, you are a witness! If you are summoned into court to tell about it, then you must choose whether or not to be an honest witness.

As a Christian, you have seen the power of what He has done in your life. You know the truth. You are commanded to tell others.

You must decide if you will be a faithful witness. Or you can choose to keep your mouth shut. Or you can even be a complete coward and deny God before scoffers — so that they don't make fun of you. If so, you are being a lying witness. You are pretending that God has done nothing for you.

And you may very well be dooming those scoffers to hell. This may be their only chance to hear the truth.

God may have sent them across your path so they can hear of His love before they meet that bullet waiting for them down the street.

You can choose.

So, shall we go unhappily forth, preaching in our own guilt and self-condemnation?

No. Read 1 Corinthians 12:1. It does not tell everybody to be medical missionaries or tent revival evangelists. But it does tell us to find out what gift God has given us — and what our job is in God's scheme of things.

I am a particularly lousy nurse. I would rather order a sick person to rise up and walk in faith and health and joy. However, if somebody treats me like that when I'm ill, I am not exactly thrilled or comforted.

So, my role on earth is not in a hospice for the terminally ill, gently and patiently helping them know the joy of the Lord as they await healing . . . or their promotion out of this painful world. My role is that of evangelist and teacher.

I have a friend whose gift is writing. He can teach more at the keyboard of a word processor than most preachers. But in the pulpit, he is disorganized and ends up telling jokes. He can't pull off a good altar call. So, he has learned to stay where God has put him — typing away on powerful books that have changed thousands of lives.

I was at a recent convention where a distributor from Australia was telling about how a young atheist had come to the Lord through a novel that this writer had edited extensively.

There were tears in the writer's eyes as he listened. Remember, this guy's name isn't on any of the books he works over for evangelists and authors whose literary talents need a little help. But as he heard about the young Aussie who now loves Jesus, my friend knew it was all worthwhile.

He knew he was doing what God wanted from him. Behind the scenes he was helping men of God speak more eloquently on the written page. He was plundering hell!

So what are you supposed to do? Find out what God requires of you! Until you get a clear focus on your life's call, just be content to talk candidly about what God has done for you. Don't be obnoxious about it, just be honest.

Sure, you can pretend that God has never done anything. But I believe you know the truth: that He has brought you through. That He has intervened on your behalf. That He has given you everything you have.

How do you talk about God to total strangers?

I believe we must constantly ask the Lord for strength and the right words to witness for Him regardless of how we feel at any given moment.

Our lifestyle of the rich and righteous must be to touch the lives of others daily.

There is no excuse for not being an obedient witness! You can always find the chance to touch someone's life — on the job, at the supermarket, in the mall, at home. Hurting people are everywhere. Nowhere in the Bible did God tell sinners to go to church. We are to go to them, not to jam religion into them, but to love them, and to help them. My job and your job is to help hurting people.

I look for them, then find ways to help them.

Once on an airplane, a flight attendant was very unpleasant. Nothing I did seemed to work as I tried to reach out to her. Finally, I gave her a five dollar bill. She said, "What is this for?"

I said, "Just a little gift. Buy yourself something or have lunch on me."

Money was so important to her that it broke down the barrier. She opened up her heart, telling me some sad things going on in her life. Later, in the airport, I led her to Christ in five minutes.

Such a change happened in her life! Her husband became a Christian. Months later my outreach's singing group, *Illustrator*, was doing a concert in the area where they lived. She and her husband took their teenagers to hear us. The kids gave their lives to Christ. The little gift was the key that unlocked the door.

You have to look for hurting people.

Figure out what they need.

Fill that gap in their lives.

How can you help your church to grow?

Here's a gap that your church can fill: Offer free baby-sitting! What? Yes, offer to pick up neighborhood urchins and take them to church on Sunday mornings. Their parents will have a good feeling in their hearts as well as a quiet morning to themselves.

And what will you be accomplishing with

these pint-sized pagans? You will be teaching these third-graders and kindergartners all about Jesus Christ. Is it worth it? Such giants of our faith as Dwight Moody and Billy Graham gave their lives to Jesus while they were still children.

If you fill these kids with a consuming passion for the lost, guess who they will work on first? Mommy and Daddy!

You can add many new families to your church by getting to the second-graders and winning the sixth-graders.

What if nonbelievers want to argue?

Remember as you work for Him, that you are told to be a witness, not a lawyer. God doesn't need an advocate. He can do that for himself, through the work of the Holy Spirit.

What He needs from you and me is someone to tell what we have seen and heard and experienced.

We plant the seed.

He will water it. He will do His own convicting and convincing.

What if your life is such a mess that you are a lousy witness?

Alas, this is a common problem in the Church.

What if your personal affairs are in such an uproar that you can't talk about God's blessings without people laughing in your face? Or behind your back?

Well, don't be so self-conscious of your failings. Nobody is perfect.

But it certainly is true that you can't be a good witness if you are in constant conflict in your relationships with your family, of if your business transactions are dishonest.

The answer, of course, is not to quit witnessing. Instead, witness more! And clean up your act at the same time. You're going to have some interesting accountability. People are going to challenge you, citing your past sins.

So, take that opportunity to apologize and make up for your dirty deeds. Then, go and try to sin no more.

It's not easy.

One day very early in my ministry, as Barb and I were on our way to meet a pastor, a man almost ran into our car. I laid on the horn. (That's what horns are for, right?) He honked back in anger. We both had to stop at the next light. When it turned green, I sped away, burning rubber, just to show him who was in charge. He shook his fist out the window.

My beautiful wife, Barb, quietly asked me if I thought I had demonstrated a Christian spirit.

My retort was that it was his fault.

A few minutes later, when we arrived at the pastor's home, who do you think answered my knock?

The pastor was the other driver.

But each of us learned a very good and embarrassing lesson.

Living a holy, righteous life isn't a cake walk.

Is an enlightened, modern Christian really supposed to live up to old Victorian taboos about premarital or extramarital sex?

Back in the days of the Early Church, there was a lot of hedonism and narcissism in the world. Naturally, when a former sex addict walked the aisle and became a member of the First Downtown Church of Corinth, he brought with him a certain amount of baggage. Such as a roving eye for the ladies. At one point, the Christians of Corinth apparently had turned their communion services into drunken brawls.

There was even a popular rationale that the more that a Christian sinned, the more wondrous grace God gave him.

The apostle Paul was stunned and shocked when he dropped in. Apparently on the long voyage to his next speaking engagement, he wrote the Christians several scathing letters. Among the gentler things he wrote are:

> . . . I am writing you that you
> must not associate with anyone who

calls himself a brother but is sexually immoral or greedy, an idolater or a slanderer, a drunkard or a swindler. With such a man do not even eat (1 Cor. 5:11;NIV).

No temptation has seized you except what is common to man. And God is faithful; he will not let you be tempted beyond what you can bear. But when you are tempted, he will also provide a way out so that you can stand up under it (1 Cor. 10:13;NIV).

Be ye not unequally yoked together with unbelievers: for what fellowship has righteousness with unrighteousness? and what communion hath light with darkness? (2 Cor. 6:14).

Without getting moralistic or stepping up into the pulpit, I think the topic of sex outside of marriage is becoming a matter of common sense. Just today, as I am working on this book, I read in the newspaper that entire countries in Africa are being decimated by the AIDS virus.

A news magazine had a lengthy article on this plague and quoted a noted medical expert. He said that there's never been a virus like this one. He says that it actually metamorphoses your body so that your body is manufacturing the millions of AIDS cells rather than fighting them off.

The result is eventual death, he said, for every known case so far. And he added that he sincerely doubted that the disease will ever be curable.

But it is preventable.

How?

Behave yourself. Of course, there are the terrible instances of the innocent being infected by tainted blood transfusions or in the womb.

But you and I can be pretty safe by only having sex with the one beloved spouse God gives us until death do us part.

Monogamy is the formal term.

Swans do it. They stay with the same mate for life.

It's time that a few Christian ugly ducklings finally turned into the beautiful swans that God intended.

What's wrong with a Christian enjoying an occasional toke of marijuana or getting a little drunk?

"Sanctify yourselves therefore, and be holy: for I am the Lord your God," says the Lord in Leviticus 20:7.

Can you be a good witness for Jesus Christ while you're getting a little high with your friends?

No. You can't straddle the fence, unless you belong to the First Church of Laodicea, those on-off, half-hearted Christians that God rebuked in Revelation. If you remember, they were on the road to hell, although they were attempting to make it look like the straight-and-narrow.

"So if the Son sets you free, you will be free indeed" (John 8:36;NIV). That means that you don't keep going back to Egypt after God has brought you through the wilderness and delivered you into the Promised Land.

Romans 6:12-13 warns, "Let don't sin therefore reign in your mortal body, that ye should obey its lusts thereof . . . . but yield yourselves unto God . . . ."

Here's another reason: "Don't you know you yourselves are God's temple and that God's Spirit lives in you? If anyone destroys God's temple, God will destroy him; for God's temple is sacred, and you are that temple" (1 Cor. 3:16-17;NIV).

"I beseech you therefore, brethren, by the mercies of God, that ye present your bodies a living sacrifice, holy, acceptable unto God, which is your reasonable service. And be not conformed to this world: but be ye transformed by the renewing of your mind, that ye may prove what is good, and acceptable, and perfect, will of God . . . . Abhor that which is evil; cleave to that which is good" (Rom. 12:1-9).

"Having therefore these promises, dearly beloved, let us cleanse ourselves from all filthiness of the flesh and spirit, perfecting holiness in the fear of God" (2 Cor. 7:1).

Is homosexuality forbidden in the Bible?

You may think that this is a rude topic for a nice Christian book. However, we live in a society where homosexuality is being offered as a legitimate alternative.

In schools, kids are being told that if they are "born gay," that there is nothing they can do about it except give in to their lusts.

However, the Bible is plain. First, there are a number of promises I've quoted several pages back that tells us God does not allow us to be tempted beyond our ability to say "no." We are always given an escape route.

Believe it or not, nobody is "born gay." That notion was popularized by newspaper advice columnists, but has no basis in fact. There are a great many cases of "gays" who have turned from the lifestyle and enjoyed normal heterosexual lifetime relationships with a devoted spouse.

Beyond that, there are some very stern commandments mandating heterosexuality and celibacy as a Christian's only options:

> Thou shalt not lie with mankind, as with womankind: it is abomination (Lev. 18:22).
>
> If a man also lie with mankind, as he lieth with a woman, both of them have committed an abomination: they shall surely be put to

death . . . (Lev. 20:13).

Professing themselves to be wise, they became fools . . . And likewise also the men . . . burned in their lust one toward another . . . . God gave them over to a reprobate mind . . . (Rom. 1:22-28).

But, you may hear, didn't you know that David and Jonathan were gay lovers? And so were the apostle Paul and young Timothy? Well, these unfortunate theories rise out of an American culture that pretends that men are not supposed to have affectionate feelings for one another.

We guys are supposed to be macho rocks of emotionless strength, such as John Wayne taking Iwo Jima single-handedly, Rocky standing triumphant in the boxing ring for the fifth time, or Charles Lindbergh flying the Atlantic alone for freedom, apple pie, and the American way.

We're taught that little boys aren't supposed to cry. Tough guys are supposed to be able to take anything. Preachers aren't supposed to be vulnerable. Policemen aren't supposed to get emotionally involved.

Baloney. I hurt and so do you. My heart goes out to people and I have to respond.

When I hurt, I am grateful when you care.

We've got to get past some incredible cultural garbage for which our language is partly to blame. "Love" is an inadequate English word for everything ranging from fatherly affection for a beautiful daughter to Christian concern for strangers.

We use it to describe devotion for our pets. And our delight with a pickup truck. Or a 64-year-old man's deep affection for his childhood buddy and lifelong fishing partner. Or a Christian girl's intense concern for her Jewish math tutor dying of cancer.

Or the wide range of my intimate affections for my wife — a wonderful woman who is everything from my best friend to my honest advisor and the one joyous playmate that my great Heavenly Father gave me for my delight.

Love, love, love.

The bottom line is that we're supposed to love one another. Guys are supposed to love guys. And gals. And old ladies. And little babies.

The Bible records that David and Jonathan enjoyed a boyhood friendship that lasted into manhood, a deep bonding that included intense loyalty and empathy. But the standards of their day would have mandated their being stoned to death had their beautiful relationship been sexual. The Old Testament is so firm about homosexuality and so candid about all of David's other sins, that it is absurd to think that a gay affair would not have been detailed unflinchingly in the Bible just as was David's affair with Bathsheba. That story is told with complete honesty — along with how God punished David.

What about Paul, who was apparently single? Young Timothy was raised by his mother and grandmother. Visiting their home, Paul apparently saw enormous potential in this godly boy. Remember the disappointment the missionary team had with another young preacher, John Mark? Perhaps Paul saw new hope for the future in this earnest young Christian.

In the Books of 1 and 2 Timothy, Paul held the Greek youngster to rigid standards of behavior and gave him a wealth of advice on everyday living. Perhaps Timothy became the son that Paul never had. But to infer anything sexual is to read fiction between the lines of the Scriptures. It simply is not there. Paul loved the boy. His affection for the kid is an extraordinary example for all of us.

To this day, a preacher's legacy is guaranteed if he is fortunate enough to be given a young Timothy.

So, is love between men forbidden?

No. If anything, it is required. But gay sexual relations bring upon us terrible curses. Heterosexual sex, on the other hand, was designed by God for our delight — and specifically to be enjoyed by one man and one woman who become one flesh for life.

Is there a spiritual gift of judgment?

This is an issue that must be addressed because contemporary ministries are such a powerful tool of evangelism. Some are being attacked.

So, when are we permitted to judge?

A mother and her child came out of church

and saw a man smoking. The mother remarked, caustically, "Look at that, just out of church, and already smoking."

The four year old beside her piped up, "Listen to that, just out of church, and already judging!"

It's really easy to criticize the dirty wash on the neighbor's line, when, in fact, it is your own dirty window. One man was criticizing his wife and I told him never ever criticize his wife's judgment — just look who she married.

There is a strong biblical injunction, "Judge not, that ye be not judged." It goes on to say that others will judge us with the same yardstick that we use.

Some criticize the pastor or other leaders in the church. They can't tell you what should be done, but they are sure that the way it is being done is wrong. They seem to be unhappy unless they are finding fault with someone or something. They are quick to tell you why they quit this or that church or job, and throw out asides in order to bring judgment on others.

James comments that no fountain can yield both salt water and sweet. How is it that the same person can both praise God and criticize his fellow Christians?

Judging others and gossip seem to go together. None of us are strangers to gossip. We have listened to it, or been on the receiving end of rumors and exaggerations, or worse yet, spread its poison.

Many times our conversation is full of judgments about things we have heard, taken as fact, and passed on without checking either for accuracy or taking into account the damage which will be done. In Proverbs 8:13, Solomon said that God hates a froward mouth. Leviticus 19:16 commands us not to go up and down as a talebearer. Psalm 101:5 tells us that God will cut off one who slanders his neighbor.

Someone asked me if I had heard about the problem of a prominent televangelist. I told him that I had, but added, "But I didn't hear about yours, yet."

Some folks seem to have to judge; they seem to feel that they have been commissioned to set standards and see that the rest of us adhere to them. They like to feel that they have the gift of judgment, and if you don't do things their way, it can't possibly be done correctly.

Often, we are very quick to judge a person who owes you money as being dishonest. We once sold a motor home to a man we thought was a friend. He cheated us of $10,000. After awhile, we said it's okay, because it is all God's anyway. God will take care of it. We forgave the man the debt. However, every once in awhile, I would think about it, and the thought would come to me, *That old buzzard will get it someday, and it will serve him right.*

The Lord showed me that I hadn't really forgiven him. My bad thoughts and judgment and condemnation of him were worse than his refusal to pay me. In Matthew 6:15, Jesus said that if we didn't forgive others, we would not be forgiven. I didn't like this Scripture at all.

Unforgiveness and judging can turn into bitterness and destroy you and others. I've been told the mass murders committed by the Charles Manson "family" originated from his bitterness toward a record producer who didn't like his music. Manson sent people to what he thought was the producer's home, not knowing that the man had moved, telling them to kill everyone.

Cults can develop when people in positions of leadership become bitter toward those in authority over them. They break from their denomination or organization, bitterly do their own thing, and in worst case scenarios, can end up like the infamous Jim Jones.

At a church where I was speaking, the pastor warned me that a certain lady would almost undoubtedly find something she didn't like to talk to me about. He said that she did that to every guest speaker.

Afterwards, as I was signing some books, she approached me and asked for a few minutes of my time. Of course, I agreed. She began by telling me how much she had enjoyed my ministry, but continued, "Do you think God wants us to waste money?"

I acknowledged, "Oh, no, I'm sure that He wants us to be good stewards with our finances."

She then went on, "What do you think He things about gold?" I knew then that she had seen my watch or my ring.

I said, "He is really into gold. He made it and evidently loved it so much that the streets of heaven are made of it! He is even letting a few folks that He can trust have a little of it down here, so that it's not so much of a shock to us when we get to heaven and see those gold streets!"

She looked at me and said, "You know, that's really nice." She looked so disarmed.

The pastor told me later that she was asking God to trust her with a little bit herself.

Criticism often comes when you obey God. The Lord told Peter to go to the Gentiles. He obeyed and went. When the church in Jerusalem heard about his crazy vision, and that he had even gone and eaten with Gentiles, their first reaction was to be critical.

The "board" went so far as to call Peter on the carpet. Fortunately for us Gentiles, when Peter explained the facts of the case, they held their peace.

It's easy to criticize when you are resistant to new ideas, and convinced that the established method is the only correct one. A dead congregation will be critical, while a live one will just rejoice that souls are getting into the family of God.

Let's be careful in our own lives that we learn to control the tendency to criticize, and to let God be the judge in all matters.

4

Are We Supposed to Shoot Our Own Wounded?

The army of God has a somewhat deserved reputation for being the only army in the world which turns its back on its own soldiers downed in spiritual battle.

Actually, it's worse than that. So many self-righteous Christians actually seem to take glee in shooting in the back — with gossip, criticism, and public denunciation — any fellow Christian who stumbles on the straight and narrow path of righteousness.

We all know that Satan's goal from the very beginning has been the destruction of Christ and His church, and that he will use any and all means to accomplish that goal. One of his slickest methods is to cause dissension and destruction from within. Why would you want to talk of bad points in someone's life anyway? Why not praise the good points or say nothing? The only thing worse than a gossiper is a listener.

The use of half-truths is one of the best devices in the enemy's arsenal. A half-truth coupled with an innuendo can quickly become an outright lie. It's possible to repeat something frequently enough that you eventually believe it. And it's possible to think things and actually believe you said them.

Consider the following situation: Your teenager is on an outing with several of his friends. He knows he is supposed to be home by 10 p.m. You know that the car he is driving is not totally reliable. When he arrives home an hour late, he tells you that the car didn't start until 15 minutes before then. What he doesn't tell you is that no one tried until then. Has he lied? No, but neither has he told you the truth. By omitting one fact, he has altered the entire story.

This often happens in more serious matters. By omitting something, or adding a doubt to a true happening, we can ruin the testimony of a brother or sister. We need to build relationships, not tear them down. Some feel if they can talk badly of someone who has fallen, or someone they don't agree with, it makes them look better.

Another weapon is to cause one of us to attack another one. If I don't like your style of music or some part of your doctrine, I can always find others who will agree with my point of view if I begin to talk about how wrong you are and how bad the thing you are doing is.

Of course, if I do this, there are others who will disagree with me, and soon we will choose sides, and each side will look for all the bad in the other side in order to make their own case look better. Nothing positive is usually accomplished. Churches split, relationships are ruined, and nothing is done for God's glory, but we are foolish in the eyes of the world.

The series of scandals which has rocked the Church was bad because of the sins involved, but much worse was the fact that the publicity surrounding them stemmed from a group of prominent televangelists publicly "blowing the whistle" on each other. They didn't care how they were all going to look to the unsaved, nor how many of the saints were going to be wounded in the crossfire.

When a baby is learning to walk, we don't knock him down because he falls the first time. When a teenager is learning to drive, we don't shoot him if he knocks over the garbage can. And if a mature adult makes an error in judgment, we don't laugh and hold him up to ridicule. We do show each one where he made his mistake and help him to try again, until he gets it right.

The apostle Peter denied Christ three times

but later went on to become one of the leaders of the Early Church. What would have happened if the rest of the Disciples had refused to accept Peter after he failed? Because Peter repented and was restored, his later ministry was more fruitful than his earlier.

I once saw a newspaper photo of a mallard duck that was flying with an arrow through its chest. The caption read, "Wounded But Still Flying."

So what do we do? Do we ignore sin in our midst? No. Do we ostracize the sinner or the fallen saint? Neither course is correct. We must learn to confront the sin without condemning the sinner.

In 1 Corinthians 10:13 we read, "Let him that think he stands take heed, lest he fall."

The motivation of most of the criticism and contention which goes on in the Church seems to be jealousy, envy, and pride. Our motivation in confrontation must be the restoration of the fallen brother. Restoration to the Lord first of all, and then restoration to the Church and to the service of the Lord. Don't kill him/her because of a fall. Love them, let God take care of them.

There are times in war when a person is wounded and he doesn't know it. Or he knows it but is so full of adrenaline that he continues to fight and causes the death of his men. He has lost credibility which is necessary for leadership in the eyes of his men. Someone has to remove him from command, before he causes a complete disaster. This can also happen in a church or ministry.

Leadership takes action in order to restore a wounded leader and help him regain his credibility.

Three precepts should be remembered: First, awareness of our own frailty; next, agreement with the law of love; and finally, accountability to God and to each other for our words and our actions.

Isn't anybody here perfect? What is sin?

"To him that knows to do good, and does it not, to him that is sin," says James 4:17.

What happens if I do not forsake my sins?

"The wages of sin are death, but the gift of God is eternal life through Jesus Christ our Lord," says Romans 6:23.

What happens if God forgives me?

"As far as the east is from the west, so far has he removed our transgressions from us," says Psalm 103:12.

"I am He who blots out your transgressions and will not remember your sins," says Isaiah 43:25.

"I have blotted out, as a thick cloud, your transgressions, and, as a cloud, your sins. Return unto me, for I have redeemed you," promises Isaiah 44:22.

"I will remember their sin no more," says Jeremiah 31:34.

"Who is like Him that can pardon sin? He retains not his anger forever, because He delights in mercy. He will turn again, He will have compassion upon us. He will subdue our iniquities and cast all our sins into the depths of he sea," assures Micah 7:18-19.

"For I will be merciful to their unrighteousness. Their sins will remember no more," says Hebrews 8:12.

What do I have to do for God to forgive me?

"**Believe** on the Lord Jesus Christ, and you must be saved, and your house," says Acts 16:31.

"Whosoever shall **confess me** before others, that person I will confess also before my Father which is in heaven. But whosoever shall deny me before men, him will I also deny before my Father which is in heaven," says Matthew 10:32-33.

"If you **confess** with your mouth the Lord Jesus, and believe in your heart that God raised Him from the dead, you will be saved. For with your heart you believe unto righteousness and with your mouth confession is made unto salvation," explains Romans 10:9-10

Is anything else expected of us? On the Day of Pentecost, here is what the apostle Peter told the thousands that they had to do: "Repent of your sins, and get baptized, every one of you in the name of Jesus Christ for the forgiveness of those sins, and you will receive the gift of the Holy Ghost," (Acts 2:38).

Do I have to get baptized?

Well, you don't have to do anything but die and pay taxes, I suppose. However, when you study the Bible and try to determine what is expected of us, occasionally, it is good to just sit back and watch what the early Christians did.

And if Jesus did something as an example for us to follow, it's a good idea to pay attention, too.

Baptism really makes no sense.

Believing makes plenty of sense. You have to believe in all this before you're going to go through with it. Repenting of your sins is downright logical. Confessing to other people is brilliant.

But getting dunked from head to foot in a tank of water or a smelly fishpond or a freezing creek really is an odd requirement.

Why did He do it?

One reason is because Jesus allowed himself to be baptized. The full story is told in Matthew 3:11, 15-16, as well as in Mark 1:8-10 and in Luke 3:16, 21-22.

Then, the story is repeated in John 1:29-34.

It would appear that this one incident was pretty important for all four of the Gospels to go into it in detail. Then, through the New Testament, new believers are always being told that it's one of the things they need to take care of.

"Don't you know, that so many of us as were baptized into Jesus Christ were baptized into his death?" says Romans 6:3.

"For as many of you as have been baptized into Christ have put on Christ" explains Galatians 3:27.

Some Christians believe baptism is vital for salvation. I see that we are told to do it.

Frankly, I am not sure that it's worth arguing about. Be on the safe side. Get it taken care of.

Does a Christian have to go to church?

Again, let's handle this one by example, because there is nowhere in the Bible that says that we have to go to Sunday school, Sunday morning worship, Sunday night Bible study, and Wednesday night prayer meeting.

Jesus attended church a lot.

"And Jesus went about all Galilee, teaching in their synagogues, and preaching the gospel of the kingdom, and healing all manner of sickness and all manner of disease among the people," says Matthew 4:23.

"And Jesus went about all the cities and villages, teaching in their synagogues, and preaching the gospel of the kingdom, and healing every sickness and every disease among the people," says Matthew 9:35.

"And when he was departed thence, he went into their synagogue," says Matthew 12:9.

"And when he was come into his own country, he taught them in their synagogue, inasmuch that they were astonished, and said, Whence has this one this wisdom, and these mighty works," records Matthew 13:54.

Why does anybody go to church?

"For where two or three are gathered together in my name, there am I in the midst of them," says Matthew 18:20. Plus, we gain strength from one another.

It's hard to stay home and watch church on TV and grow in the Lord. You need to fellowship.

You need to have Christian friends.

You'll find them at church.

5

Can We Clean Our Fish Before Catching Them?

**What are we supposed
to do about people who
continue to sin?**

It does no good to try to clean and scale a
fish while it is still swimming around in the river.
Likewise, it's useless to try to reform a sinner while
he is still a sinner.

Many a person has been driven away from
the church because they were told to quit this or

that. Neither drinking, cursing, smoking, or adultery will send someone to hell. When someone accepts Christ into his/her life, those things fall off. God cleans the "fish."

We seem to try to treat the symptoms instead of the disease. A child can't run before he learns to walk. A set of rules is like putting a band-aid on a severed artery. It doesn't do the job.

If we are on an airplane flight and smoke begins to fill the cabin, the smoke is not really the problem. It is only the visible evidence of a serious problem.

Likewise, drugs in themselves are only a symptom of the problem. The problem is the inability to cope with a life without Christ, filled with pressures, loneliness, and emptiness.

Abortion is not the problem. The loss of moral values that plagues our nation is the problem. Abortion is only another of the symptoms.

Neither is pornography the problem. Nor is homosexuality. Nor is premarital sex. They all are just serious symptoms of man's sin. The problem is rebellion against the laws of a holy God.

People without Jesus are the problem, and only by showing them that you care and that God cared enough to send His Son, Jesus, and that Jesus cares, will they be reached. Fighting evil and injustice are not bad, but that will not bring people to Jesus.

In my witnessing to people, I try to adapt to them and their circumstances. To a teenager, I talk music or sports. To a trucker, I talk trucks. To a pilot, I talk airplanes. If I am talking to an intellectual, I have to wing it. I've talked politics, fishing, travel, and cars. I have laughed and joked. If I don't know anything about a subject, I ask questions.

When my "fish" finds out that I am a minister, his first reaction is usually disbelief. I'm frequently told, "You're too happy to be a minister."

You won't win people by beginning with a list of their problems. They usually know that they are in bad shape without being reminded. Begin by dealing with them in their comfort zone.

If you are at an accident scene, and you see a victim lying on the ground, badly mangled, you don't kneel beside him and begin telling him how bad he looks, and that you think he might not make it. Instead, you speak words of hope, comfort, and encouragement, while you send someone for medical help.

When you are talking with an unbeliever, be sure that you are speaking English, and not "Christian-ese." "Praise the Lord" and "Hallelujah" can scare some people so badly that they forget the rest of what you said. It's like throwing rocks into the water to let the fish know you're coming.

A circuit riding preacher in the last century had a horse who had been trained to respond to certain religious clichés. "Praise the Lord" made him go, and "Amen" made him stop. He sold the horse to a prospector, and carefully explained to him the system that the horse was used to. One day, the horse got spooked and began to run away. The prospector hollered, "Whoa!" but the horse didn't understand "whoa" and continued toward the cliff. Just in the nick of time, the prospector remembered and yelled, "Amen." The horse stopped right on the edge of the cliff. As he wiped the sweat off his forehead, the man breathed, "Praise the Lord."

And off the cliff he went.

Your religious clichés may also push some-one over the edge.

Are we servants or masters?

Jesus himself actually became a servant while He was here on earth. We should follow His example. The world laughed at William Booth of the Salvation Army when he placed soup kitchens on London's street corners and began feeding the homeless, drunkards, and down-and-outers. But it won the hearts of people, and many found Christ. He didn't talk about how bad these people were, he served them, and won them to Christ.

Being a servant is also a good principle for marriages. If you want a great marriage, be ser-vants to each other, always looking out for your mate. Paul urged husbands to love their wives even as they love themselves, and wives to reverence their husbands (Eph. 5:21-33). God knew that if a man would love, the wife would willingly follow him, and that the children would follow this kind of an example willingly.

For the last 2,000 years Christians have failed to win the world because they have not followed Christ's instruction to "go . . . into all the world and preach the gospel." Preaching the gospel is fishing. You catch them, let God clean them.

You can also congratulate people on what they have done well, like long years of marriage, a job well done, or a promotion. Many good people will go to hell — they need Christ.

I never tear down a person's religious house. I just build a better one next door, and get him to move into it. If we are discussing denominations or organizations, I let them know that it's not the label we put on ourselves — Baptist or Methodist or Catholic or Assemblies of God or Brethren or whatever — but it's a living relationship with Jesus Christ that makes the difference.

The Bill Haldeman family are friends of mine and of our ministry. One day I called Bill to meet me at the airport and have lunch with me during a layover on my way through. We decided not to eat at the airport, but to go to a restaurant nearby.

We drove around for a few minutes, turning from one street to another with no particular place in mind, and neither of us was familiar with the area. Finally, we saw a "Popeye's Chicken" shop and decided to eat there, although we could see that we were not in the best neighborhood in town.

After we had ordered our dinners and were waiting for them, an old, poorly dressed woman approached our table and asked to have our coffee cream, if we didn't want it. We gave her the little cups, and she took them to another table and drank them.

In order to touch people's lives, you have to keep your eyes open. We decided to buy her a dinner, so I ordered and Bill paid for it. She was very thankful. I began to talk to her lightly about her smoking, stressing that she was hurting her health. She agreed. I then worked the conversation around so that it was about the Lord. In a few minutes, in a very quiet way, sitting right there in a booth, she accepted Christ into her life.

Bill and I returned to our own dinners, and began to discuss the things of God. A man, possibly in his late fifties, who was sitting nearby, listened for a few minutes, then came over to our table. He apologized for intruding and asked if he could just sit where he could hear better. We began to share with him, and in a few minutes he also accepted Christ.

Sometimes you have to win people to you before you can win them to Christ. Your life should be so transparent that Jesus can be seen through you.

Because the man said that he didn't own a Bible, I asked for his name and address. He knew the woman who we had led to Christ. When I returned home, I sent each of them a Bible and some copies of my book, *God's Got Your Number,* to give away in the housing project where they lived. We have been in contact with him since that time.

As Bill and I left the restaurant, I said, "Wow, what are the odds of leading two people to Christ during lunch!"

Bill's comment was, "With you, 100 percent."

Our job is to touch lives, to catch fish. If you're going to fish, you have to think like a fish. To be a fisher of men, think like the people you want to win. Don't throw out rules to frighten them either, like go to church, pay tithes, wear a longer dress, take this off, put this on. Let God do the cleaning.

In Matthew 22:9-10, Jesus told us in the parable of the wedding feast to go out and bring everyone, both the good and the bad. Somehow, people find all kinds of excuses not to fish.

Peter, James, and John all went up on the mountain with Jesus. God's glory came down, and Peter really got excited and thought a building program was the answer. Not just one building, but three, so that each of them could have one.

But Jesus was more concerned about healing a young demon-possessed child. The work of winning souls is more important than any building program. Churches get so concerned about location and the facility that they forget to care for the needs of the lost.

When things are truly happening, people will find a church even if it doesn't have a great location. Parking problems can also be overcome, when the congregation and the leadership really care about souls. I know several churches which shuttle folks (regular members) for a mile or so in order to leave sufficient parking on their lots for visitors. Our pastor calls this the "fellowship shuttle" and insists that it is a good way to meet and make friends. It works.

When a store is having a real sale, like $500 microwaves for $99, people will find that store; even if it means getting lost several times and driving miles out of the way.

Now don't misquote me and say that I don't believe in church building programs. I know that they are necessary, but we must never lose sight that the main reason a local church exists is in order to meet needs in the community.

Bill and I laughed and rejoiced as we drove back to the airport. This type of thing happens to me frequently, and it can happen to anyone. But you have to stay alert, keep your eyes open, and look for troubled people. God will use you if you let Him. Your job is to touch lives. You are to be a fisherman. Let God take care of the cleaning.

6

Many Curse God and Jesus, but Few the Holy Spirit — Why Not?

What is blasphemy?

Miriam, the sister of Moses, was stricken with leprosy because she criticized Moses (Num. 21). Jesus warned that blasphemy against the Holy Ghost would never be forgiven after His critics had accused Him of doing miracles by the power of

Satan (Matt. 12:31-32 and Mark 3: 28-29).

From these examples, we must come to the conclusion that God feels very strongly about criticizing those whom He has called to a special ministry — so strongly that He will not forgive the sin of imputing to Satan those things which are the work of the Holy Spirit. This is serious.

In the last several years there has been much controversy over new methods of evangelism and worship. Some prominent ministers have been extremely vocal with their criticism of those things of which they did not approve. They have gone so far as declaring that the unfamiliar methods were satanic.

It's extremely easy to disapprove of things which we don't like, which are unfamiliar, or which we don't understand. This is human nature.

A person who attended a concert and didn't like the style of music said that it was of Satan, even though more than 200 kids accepted Christ. (Surely Satan didn't convert them.) When the comment was made that it was wonderful to see all these conversions, her response was that "they should have been saved some other way."

Most of us tend to resist change. This may not be all bad. To accept new things without looking at them carefully and considering them in the light of Scripture can be just as dangerous as refusing to consider them at all. The proper way to consider new ideas is with the Bible and a lot of prayer and an open mind.

Both Miriam and the Pharisees had a knowl--

edge of the things of God. God requires more of those who know than He does of those who are ignorant. Jesus said, "For unto whomsoever much is given, of him shall much be required" (Luke 12: 48).

We are also warned not to offend those who are weak in the faith (Matt. 18:6; Rom. 14:15). It grieves God's heart when one ministry fights another. It hurts when a ministry says another ministry is an enemy of the Church. The Scripture gives stern warning to people who slander and cause discord.

What criteria can we use then to decide about these things? First and foremost, does the method stand the test of Scripture by bringing glory to God? Are people coming to know the Lord? Are they being made stronger in their faith?

Next, what is the lifestyle of the ministers (i.e., preachers, musicians, etc.)? Does it glorify God, and are they morally pure? I'm not saying that we can expect perfection from anyone, but does there seem to be a desire to walk and live as Jesus did? Do they lift up Christ? Then, does the message conform to the Scripture?

Finally, what do we do if we feel that something or someone does not stand up to those tests?

First, pray earnestly that God will deal with the situation. Then guard your tongue carefully, remembering that attributing to Satan those things which are the work of the Holy Spirit is a very dangerous thing and could cost you heaven.

The best advice ever given about this kind

of a situation was spoken by Gamaliel to the Sanhedrin.

"Refrain from these men, and leave them alone: for if this counsel or this work be of men, it will come to nothing: but if it be of God, ye cannot overthrow it; lest happily ye be found even to fight against God" (Acts 6:38-39).

Can a Christian get away with a little fib?

God forgives. But if we make a mess, sometimes He makes us sit in it for a while.

"I have hated them that regard lying vanities," warns Psalm 31:6.

"The lip of truth shall be established for ever: but a lying tongue is but for a moment," says Proverbs 12:19.

"Put away lying. Speak truth to your neighbor. For we are all in this together," proclaims Ephesians 4:25.

And here's something that we all have to watch: don't exaggerate. If you were an 11-year-old kid who occasionally smoked a little marijuana when Jesus found you, don't embellish the story.

Don't testify that you were a major crack dealer that God rescued from life in federal prison.

Your testimony is a precious thing. Don't mess it up with lies. Whatever happened to you is a good enough story.

There's a prominent Christian musician, Chris Christian, whose testimony goes something like this:

"Well, I guess you are expecting me to tell you that I was heavily into drugs and the occult and weird stuff before I found Jesus Christ and He saved me and turned my rotten life around . . . but actually, I can't remember when I wasn't a Christian.

"I was raised in a godly home by my parents and I gave my life to Jesus when I was just a little guy and I didn't go through any of that other stuff, praise God!

What if your testimony is undramatic and unexciting?

Maybe you need to use something else to talk about Jesus.

Sometimes you have to make an opening to speak. Other times, God provides opportunity. When I fly on crowded airplanes in bad weather, people are ready to hear about God.

I know God is with me, so I'm not concerned about the weather. I know He controls the wind and rain. I have flown hundreds of thousands of miles — to most parts of the world — and we have always had a safe flight. So, I talk to the others who are worried. I explain that perfect love casts out our fears, and that if they will trust God, they don't have to be afraid.

I can tell fearful fellow travelers that God is in control.

Once, flying to Alaska with a bunch of fishermen, a man asked me what I did for a living.

I told him that I was a professional fisherman. He asked if I planned to fish in Alaska. I said that I did, and that I had ways of catching the big ones. He was very interested and asked me how big was the biggest fish I had ever caught.

I told him 275 pounds.

He asked what I did with it.

I said that I helped him go back to live with his wife in Texas.

The man looked at me blankly and said that he didn't understand.

I told him that Christ said He would make us fishers of men and that's what I fished for — men.

I began to explain what I did and what my life was about. He asked me if I was fishing right then.

I grinned the obvious answer. You can rest assured I was.

Winning folks to Christ has often been compared to fishing. Jesus said in Matthew 4:19 to Peter and Andrew, "Follow me, and I will make you fishers of men."

Fishermen are not noted for their maturity, only their fishing. Only catching fish makes you a fisherman — not the size of your boat, the cost of your pole, or the best equipment. The style of your clothing doesn't matter much either, as long as you catch fish.

I've also told people who ask what I do that I'm with the CIA (Christians in Action) on a secret mission, that I reroute traffic, that I'm an investigator, that I deal in insurance and assurance, that I have a home improvement company. Then I go on to explain these things.

It's only a way to open the door. Even a small star shines bright in the darkness.

Does God have a sense of humor?

He puts up with us, doesn't He? He loves us amid all our foolishness — He must have a good sense of humor. I believe He does.

He gave us wit. He gave us an ability to make the best of adversity. That takes a sense of humor. And we are made in His image.

There are a number of times in the Bible when it appears as if God laughs at man's foolish foibles.

"He laughs" at our threats of war against Him, says Job 41:29.

"The kings of the earth set themselves against the Lord, and against His anointed, saying, 'Let us break their bands asunder, and cast away their cords from us.' But He who sits in the heavens laughs at them," says Psalm 2:1-4.

God takes pleasure in us.

"The Lord takes pleasure in those who fear him, in those who hope in His mercy," says Psalm 147:11.

"For the Lord takes pleasure in his people. He will beautify the meek with salvation," says Psalm 149:4.

"You are worthy, O Lord, to receive glory and honor and power. For You have created all things, and for your pleasure they are and were created," proclaims Revelation 4: 11.

What can you and I do to bring pleasure to God?

"I have no pleasure in the death of the wicked," says God in Ezekiel 33:11, "but that the wicked turn and live. Turn from your evil ways!"

"Fear not, for it is your Father's good pleasure to give you the kingdom," says Luke 12:32.

"For it is God which works in you to do his good pleasure," says Philippians 2:13.

Just remember that God is God. He's not some slap-happy old geezer. He is the eternal Creator, your mighty Father, the greatest force in the universe, the One who sees all and knows all.

He deserves reverence. He is worthy of our worship and our praise and our gratitude.

So, don't let me diminish His greatness by suggesting that He has a sense of humor. I believe He does. I believe He gave me my oddball sense of humor and likes my jokes. Even my silly ones.

You've probably heard the joke about ol' Frank who always caught fish. When no one else was bringing in fish, ol' Frank would always bring home his limit.

One day the game warden went fishing with him to see why. As they got the little boat out in the middle of the lake, Frank reached into his tackle box and pulled out a stick of dynamite, lit it, and threw it into the water. After the explosion, he took out his net and started to bring the stunned fish into the boat.

The game warden was very upset and began yelling at ol' Frank and telling him how illegal this was, and that it couldn't be done this way. Frank reached into his box, calmly picked up another stick of dynamite, lit it, and handed it to the game warden. As the stunned game warden sat there watching the fuse burn, ol' Frank said, "You gonna sit there, or you gonna fish?"

This is what God is asking His children — who are supposed to be out in the world winning the lost!

**What if our own
problems are too big
for us to worry about
people going to hell?**

Do I really need to answer that?

It's this simple: Are you going to sit there or are you "gonna fish?"

7

Does God Ever Let Us Take a Vote on How He's Going to Do Things?

What is success?

It seems in life that the majority, the crowd, the biggest, the one with the most votes, rules.

However, this is not always true.

You are right when you do what God has called you to do. He has called each of us to do something.

If you want ice cream, you don't buy it at the lumber yard, you buy it where they sell ice cream.

If you want God's blessings, you do what God has called you to do.

Let's look at success. What is real success? Success is different things to different people. To a truck driver, maybe success is a new truck with lots of chrome. To a home builder, maybe success is a model home. I believe success is knowing what God wants you to do, and then doing it.

Some people have wanted success and financial freedom, not to be greedy, but so they could bless God's work. They have right and good motives for wanting to be successful financially. Always remember, no one can make you a failure without your consent.

8

Does the Majority Rule?

**What does God want
you to do?**

First, when you accept Jesus Christ as Lord
of your life, you have automatically joined the
force of soul winners. Next, you have to decide
what you are going to do about this. The majority
will follow the crowd which does little or nothing.
The trouble with doing nothing is that you never
know when you are finished.

In the days ahead, I believe many things will
change in our society. We must never change our

principles, but sometimes methods have to change if we are going to keep current and get the job done.

In the past, things were the way they were, and that was the way it was, and it couldn't be changed, at least in the thinking of a lot of people. Now, God is raising up some new folks, and not all of them young, who are tired of letting things go by. These people may be in the minority, but they want to change their world. They want to touch lives, help people, heal hurts, make things happen.

There are two kinds of people: those on the building crew and those on the wrecking crew. Those on the wrecking crew are a negative force; they breed discouragement, they are prophets of gloom, they tear down, they destroy dreams, they are dedicated agitators, always finding fault with everything. No church or pastor needs them. They are like a bad apple in a box of good ones. They will destroy others.

Those on the building crew are a positive force; they breed encouragement, they are prophets of sunshine, they are dream builders, they are dedicated faith people, givers, always looking for and finding ways to bless others. Churches, pastors, and our world in general, need them.

The builders look on the positive side. I've always liked the story of the hitchhiker wearing one shoe who was picked up. As he got into the car, the driver remarked, "What's the matter, lose a shoe?"

"No," the man answered, "found one."

I recently read an article in a magazine

titled, "Can U.S. Cars Make a Comeback?" Well, I've been seeing soul-winning people make a comeback. I used to think that Christians didn't really want to win people. Now I believe that most of them want to, but they don't know how. They like to come see an evangelist or pastor win them, but they don't really believe that they can be a soul winner.

When Mike Tyson, world heavyweight champion, boxed James "Buster" Douglas in Tokyo, the majority said that Tyson would win without a question. People who normally gamble on fights didn't, because they were so sure that Douglas would not win. But it proved to be one of the biggest upsets in boxing history. Douglas won and gained the title. The majority was wrong.

A lot of people laughed when Ronald Reagan first decided to run for president. An actor and a movie star? No way! But he made it. And whoever heard of a peanut farmer from Georgia named Jimmy Carter? Eventually, we all did. George Bush and Dan Quayle were not thought of as a winning ticket either, but look what happened.

Many of the greatest accomplishments in history happened in situations where "majority" did not rule. The odds were seemingly impossible. Columbus, Helen Keller, George Washington Carver, and Harlan Sanders all were in the minority.

Abraham Lincoln was raised on several small farms. His formal education was limited to one year. He was self-educated. However, he had a very strong desire to learn. As a boy he would walk for miles to borrow a book. He studied law, passed the bar exam, and entered politics. Abraham Lincoln had many major public defeats, and gained the reputation of being a "born loser." But he proved the majority wrong and became the sixteenth president of the United States of America. Lincoln brought our nation through some of its darkest hours. He refused to give up the struggle to save the nation. Even though it eventually cost him his life, he refused to detour although his views often belonged to the minority.

George Washington was raised in very comfortable surroundings, and enjoyed benefits as a gentleman farmer on an 8,000-acre estate which he inherited from his half-brother. He attended school from age seven through fifteen. He entered politics through his military career.

As a leader of the Continental Forces during the American Revolution, Washington lost many battles and, along with his men, suffered through the rugged winter of 1777-78 at Valley Forge. Yet, because of his leadership, America was actually birthed. Although they shared no common background, George Washington and Abraham Lincoln both had courage and integrity. Both became great leaders. They both had perseverance.

Sometimes the turtle wins the race; however, true perseverance isn't quite that simple, because there must also be determination to carry on, even when all hope seems gone. Both men had their share of setbacks, and seemed not to be in the majority. Each faced public criticism.

They were both men of prayer, if historians are to be believed.

Lincoln prayed constantly.

Look at the results.

Majority does not always rule.

Is praying without ceasing realistic?

"Watch therefore, and pray always, that you may be accounted worthy to escape all these things that shall come to pass," says Luke 21:36.

"Praying always with all prayer and supplication in the Spirit," says Ephesians 6:18.

"We give thanks to God and the Father of our Lord Jesus Christ, praying always for you," says Colossians 1:3.

"Pray without ceasing," proclaims 1 Thessalonians 5:17. Well, what does that mean? Are we all to become monks in a dark cave praying 20 hours a day?

No. That verse means we're supposed to pray about everything. If you are having a difficult time, ask the Lord to give you peace. Then, as things bother you, ask Him to show you what's wrong and what you're to do about it.

We're not supposed to conquer life's challenges in our own strength! We need the Lord! And He's always there. If we unceasingly seek His assistance, He unceasingly responds.

Sure, He sometimes tells us no, when we do

nutty things, such as lay hands on somebody else's Ferrari and claim it in faith, believing.

But He is there to supply all of our needs. Nothing is too big for Him.

Are you worried about America? About the decay of the cities? About the problems of trade imbalance and drugs and moral decadence? Well, guess what — you may be a bigger part of the solution than you suspect.

"If my people, which are called by my name, shall humble themselves, and pray, and seek my face, and turn from their wicked ways; then will I hear from heaven, and will forgive their sin, and will heal their land," promises 2 Chronicles 7:14.

Will God give you wisdom? "Call unto Me, and I will answer you, and show you great and mighty things, which you know not," promises Jeremiah 33:3.

"Whatsoever you shall ask in prayer, believing, you shall receive," says Matthew 21:22.

"Whatever things you desire, when you pray, believe that you receive them, and you shall have them," says Mark 11:24.

"The eyes of the Lord are over the righteous, and His ears are open unto their prayers," promises 1 Peter 3:12.

"And this is the confidence that we have in Him that, if we ask anything according to His will, He hears us: And if we know that He hears us, whatsoever we desired of Him," says 1 John 5:14-15.

What if I am too weak to be a good prayer warrior?

Listen, your strength is a matter between you and the Lord. He is the only one who can give you strength. And remember that He is fair. He understands. He made you.

"For He knows our makeup; He remembers that we are dust," assures Psalm 103:14.

"Say to them that are of a fearful heart, Be strong, fear not: behold, your God will come with vengeance. He will come and save you," says Isaiah 35:3-4. And He will make you strong.

"He gives power to the faint and to those who have no might. He increases their strength. Sometimes, the youths shall faint and be weary, and the young men shall fall. But they that wait upon the Lord shall renew their strength. They shall mount up with wings as eagles. They shall run, and not be weary. They shall walk, and not faint," declares Isaiah 40:29-31.

"Let the weak say, I am strong," challenges Joel 3:10.

Does God give Christians special treatment?

"You are a chosen generation, a royal priesthood, a holy nation, a peculiar people. Show forth the praises of Him who has called you out of darkness into His marvelous light," says 1 Peter 2:9.

"God is no respecter of persons," Peter told a Roman official once. "But in every nation he that fears Him, and works righteousness, is accepted with Him." (Acts 10:34-35).

God made you special. And as a Christian, He treats you special.

When He made you, incidentally, He made only one with your personality in the entire world. You can use that personality to touch the lives of others. You may not do it the way I do it, or the way someone else does it, but You can do it. God is just waiting to help you touch lives.

What is the key to success?

Believe in God, then in yourself. You can't believe in yourself without first believing in God. Jim Agard says that truly to believe in other people, you must believe in God and yourself first.

Did you know that it is aerodynamically impossible for a bumblebee to fly? The wings are too small to lift that large a body. But no one ever had a bumblebee convention or seminar to explain to the bumblebee that it couldn't be done, so he flies anyway.

Don't program yourself to fail. Even if you are sure you are in the minority, you can climb over failures and reach an altitude of answers. You can succeed in your efforts for God. Forget who or what is minority or majority. God made you to be a success, not a failure.

9

Why Can't All Christians Agree With Each Other?

Why are there so many doctrines?

It's an easy thing to turn personal preferences into doctrine with no real Scripture to back it up. When an idea or a method is new or different from what we are used to, it is not automatically either right or wrong just because it is new or different.

Possibly because I was raised inland, and

just naturally resist trying new foods, I hate oysters. I don't like the way they look, and I'm sure I wouldn't like the way they taste. But Mel Hurst, a really good friend of mine frequently eats them raw. I can't imagine him doing such a thing, but then he eats a lot of things that I don't like. Overseas, I've seen him try a lot of different foods. Mel always tries to get me to eat things I don't like. He thinks because he likes them, I will.

But this preference in food with Mel and me has never come between our relationship. We could look at a lot of things like this. Why do we try to force our preferences on others?

In the last few years, there have been quite a number of innovations in methods, including the use of drama, new styles of music, different styles of worship, and new methods of child evangelism.

Drama seems to be okay on Easter or Christmas, but not other times in the same churches. Some full-time Christian drama groups have drawn heavy criticism. Body builders and martial arts demonstrations also touch lives but draw criticism.

There are those who say that contemporary Christian music is wrong because it sounds like the world, and the music of the world appeals to the "flesh," with the connotation that it is sexually lustful.

Does God hate loud music?

Well, what did believers do in the Bible?

"And they sang together praising and giving thanks unto the Lord; because He is good, for His mercy endures for ever toward Israel," says Ezra 3:11.

But that could have been a sedate hymn, I suppose.

"Sing forth the honor of His name. Make His praise glorious," orders Psalm 66:2.

Does glorious mean loud?

"I will praise the name of God with a song, and will magnify Him with thanksgiving," says Psalm 69:30.

Does magnify mean loud?

"Sing, O you heavens. Shout, you lower parts of the earth. Break forth into singing, you mountains, O forest, and every tree therein," says Isaiah 44:23.

Ah, yes. Shout means loud.

"And with them Heman and Jeduthun with trumpets and cymbals for those that should make a sound, and with musical instruments which I made, said David, to praise therewith" (1 Chron. 23:5).

It's getting louder and louder!

"It came even to pass, as the trumpeters and singers were as one, to make one sound to be heard in praising and thanking the Lord; and when they lifted up their voice with the trumpets and cymbals and instruments of music, and praised the Lord, saying, For He is good; for His mercy endures for ever. That then the house was filled with a cloud, even the house of the Lord" (2 Chron. 5:13).

Mercy! It sounds to me as if the Lord likes loud music!

"O clap your hands, all you people; shout unto God with the voice of triumph," says Psalm 47:1.

Enough said? Well, let's not forget: "Make a joyful noise unto the Lord, all you lands. Serve the Lord with gladness. Come before His presence with singing. Enter into His gates with thanksgiving, and into His courts with praise. Be thankful unto Him, and bless His name" (Ps. 100:1-4).

So, apparently we can get away with loud.

But what about lustful? I know of no contemporary Christian music groups that encourage a lustful response. If they mean "flesh" in the nonspiritual human perspective, then all music appeals to the "flesh," which is our human side.

Is contemporary Christian music wrong?

Is there a difference between the music of people like Dave Boyer and Steve Green, which is patterned in the Frank Sinatra style; or Jimmy Swaggart, which is frequently Jerry Lee Lewis style; or Stryper, because it is in the style of heavy metal head-bangers?

None of the Christian musicians that I know is trying to promote the same things as His "worldly" counterparts. None of the Christian musicians is living the same lifestyle as his "worldly" counterpart.

If we were to take all the "fleshly" side out, there would be no Christian music of any kind. From the staid Gregorian chants to the classical hymns to the gospel songs of a generation ago, on through the range of contemporary Christian music, there is a beauty which appeals to the ear, which is part of our flesh. The style which is favored by each of us is simply a matter of personal preference.

Romans 12:1-2 commands us not to conform to this world. Critics of contemporary Christian music say that the entire art form of contemporary Christian music is very conformed to the world because of the look of the performers. But God told Samuel that he looks on the heart, not on outward appearance. We should have the mind of God in all we do, and if God does not judge by appearance, we have no right to do so.

Because man does look on the outward appearance, I agree that the principles of moderation and modesty should be observed. Some who are young and immature may push the limits of what is acceptable as to mode of dress and so on. But, if we treat them gently with a spirit of love, and allow them some time to grow up instead of harshly condemning them, they may eventually achieve a balance. I've seen this happen many times. Then again, here is where accountability comes in.

God hates the mindset of judging by appearance (James 2:1-8). There is really no such thing as a "spiritual" look.

There are groups of believers who cling to a mode of dress which has not changed since their particular part of the church was formed, some of them for as much as 350 years, some as recently as the 1940s. Being "out of style" is no indicator of spirituality.

When we are at home we attend the Stone Church, which was the first church of it's denomination in the area. It is over 60 years old and very well established.

But it is also a church which is growing and reaching out to the community. The pastor, Dale Carpenter, has the philosophy that it's not necessary to duplicate what another church is doing, but that you find a need and fill it.

Pastor Carpenter himself is a man who loves people. Although his own tastes are quite traditional, he is open to what is happening in the Church world. He has the policy that if the only ministries which he brings into the church are his personal likes, then the church will get lopsided.

So the church has standard style evangelists. It is extremely generous to missions. And it has a strong Sunday school busing program as well as jail and rest home ministries. It uses a worship team and projected song lyrics as well as standard hymns. It runs half-minute and minute spot messages on TV. It also sponsors a puppet ministry at the state fair.

It has a strong music department which does one all-out Christmas production at a local theater every year. And the youth department sponsors everything from car washes and coffee at highway rest stops to Christian rock festivals. I could add a lot more ministries of this church.

Are all those things the pastor's personal preference? No, they are not. But each one of them ministers to a segment of the community and of the local church, and are winning souls.

Many Christian leaders have been teaching that this newer, popular method of worship using Christian music, drama, athletic demonstrations, etc., are biblically unsound. These teachings have been widely accepted and have caused some division in the Christian community.

Some parents and pastors have been tempted to follow this reasoning: "These men are men of God, and they say these things are bad. I don't like these things either, so they must know what they are talking about. Therefore, the Bible backs me up when I say these things are wrong."

If this principle that new is wrong and the established is right were completely true, Martin Luther would have been burned at the stake, and the Reformation would never have taken place.

The Bible does not back up the condemnation of contemporary Christian ministries. The idea behind Christian music is to set scriptural principles to music, therefore, all Christian music should have the same purpose as the Scripture.

We are taught in 1 Timothy 3:16 that the Scripture is profitable for doctrine, for reproof, for instruction in righteousness, and for correction. Christian music should also teach, reprove, correct, and encourage Christians to be righteous.

Not all groups will cover all things in the lyrics of their songs any more than all preachers will preach on all things. Some will specialize in prophecy or faith or healing or holiness or whatever.

The Scripture is not limited to just bringing the believer into worship, and neither is Christian music. It can be a sword that cuts at the sin in our lives. It can be a balm to heal our hurts. It can be a teacher to convince the non-believer.

Then there is the myth of the "demonic beat." This is really just a smoke screen to add to a weak argument based upon personal taste. The stories of African Christians who are offended by the music may result from cultural teaching.

In some African tribes a woman must cover her ankles, but she may be bare from the waist up. Many American Christians are aghast at the European idea that wine with meals is acceptable. Ministers in some countries find it difficult to believe that some American ministers play golf. We need real biblical answers to such problems, and not just accept or reject them based on our own culture.

It has only been a few generations since the concept of Sunday school came into acceptance. When these were first started, the idea met with great resistance from the majority of the church leaders. The idea behind them was to teach children who had to work six days a week in factories how to read, using the Bible as a textbook. We now consider the Sunday school a very necessary arm of the church.

These same principles of acceptance should apply to ministries which do not fall into the pattern of a standard three hymns, prayer, offering, sermon, benediction church service.

A few years ago the band and I were participants at a festival, along with several other ministries. One of the other groups was a small circus. My first thought upon hearing this was that God has enough clowns, what does He need with a circus?

Unfortunately, I voiced this in half-jest to several people. But my curiosity got the best of me, and besides that, they were set up about 30 feet from the front of our coach. So I decided to go watch them.

To my amazement, all of the performers were very professional. There were jugglers, a tight rope act, an aerialist, and several others. At the end of each act, the performer took a few minutes to give a personal testimony.

About halfway through, God spoke to my heart. He let me know that this was only another piece of "bait," just like the music of our band. He reminded me that fishermen don't fry worms, or make sandwiches out of them; they don't even have to like worms. They do use them to catch fish.

I eventually went to the leader of the group and apologized for my previous attitude, and also publicly at the festival in front of the entire crowd.

The Scripture teaches moderation, modesty, tolerance in matters not essential to sound doctrine, and above all else, love.

Jesus said, "By this shall all men know that ye are My disciples, that ye have LOVE one for another." So if you desire to be known as His follower, follow the "better way" Paul describes in 1 Corinthians 13.

If we have preferences, because of our background or personal tastes, let's keep it to ourselves and not hinder those who could be won through a method we don't like or approve of. After all, if God uses them and is blessing them, who are we to condemn them?

A farmer was harvesting wheat. He had worked all night by the headlights on the tractor and was tired and dirty.

A traveler called to him. "Excuse me," he said, "I need directions."

The farmer ignored him, so over the noise of the machinery, he shouted his request a second time.

The farmer still ignored him. He thought that the farmer was very rude, so he started back to his car. He then noticed dark clouds on the horizon, and realized why the farmer didn't have time for him.

He wasn't going to allow anything to interrupt him until the wheat was harvested, because a storm was coming.

If we are busy working to get the harvest in, we won't have any time left to argue over preference, quarrel about minor points of doctrine, or fight over church policies.

The storm is coming, and the harvest must be gathered.

10

Is It Finally Time for Some Radical Christianity?

We need the mind of God in all we do. We need to know what God wants us to do. If you are unsure of what your call is, you are in trouble. We can't be unsure of our identity in Christ, or of what God wants us to do, if we plan to help people.

God calls some to be pastors, evangelists, missionaries, street workers, rescue mission workers, ministers of music or drama, or children's or youth workers. Some are radical in what they do.

You can't go anywhere until you decide

where it is you want to go. When you're sure of what direction you're supposed to go, or what you're to do, it will show as you do it. The call of God on your life will help give you confidence as you do the job.

But what if you don't feel any specific ministry? What do you do then?

The old proverb says to "bloom where you are planted." And the Scripture tells us "Whatsoever thy hand finds to do, do it with all your might" (Eccles. 9:10).

What will people think and say? That doesn't really matter. What does matter is that your life is holy and that you are doing what God asks of you. No one ever kicks a dead dog (or bothers to criticize someone who does nothing).

Jesus healed the sick, but He did it on the wrong day and in the wrong way in the eyes of the religious leaders of that time. Jericho was not the place where ministry took place, but Jesus ministered there. He didn't wear a blue Pharisaic robe, but a mod seamless one. He even ate with publicans and sinners. He was severely criticized for His lifestyle. Criticism is one of Satan's weapons to discourage you.

Satan will use anything he can to mess you up as you try to touch the lives of people. My wife tore her nylons just before church. She was upset, and I made the mistake of suggesting that she go without them. Now we are leaving the motel room to share Christ with a crowd of people, but our attitudes were far from good. I really didn't feel much like going to church, I felt more like killing rabbits. Satan knows what buttons to push.

A man asked his neighbor, who faithfully attended church, "I have asked you to go fishing with me several times. Why haven't you ever asked me to go to church with you?"

The Christian's chagrined reply was, "I didn't think you would be interested."

Don't rely on your feelings, or prejudge people. Do what the Lord has commanded: "Compel them to come in" (Luke 14:23).

The story is told of a man who preached in a small church in the outback of Australia. There were no converts, but as he was leaving town, a small boy asked him if he could help him find Jesus. He took the time to do it.

The preacher left town feeling very downhearted, since the meeting seemed to be a failure. Some 20 years later he returned to Australia, and was invited to sit on the platform at one of the largest crusades ever held in the area.

When the evangelist rose to speak, his first statement was, "Let me introduce you to the man who took time many years ago to lead a small boy to Christ." The smiling evangelist then introduced the surprised preacher. We often have no idea what the results of our labors really are.

Each of us has a ministry. The same chapter which lists the ministries of apostle, prophet, teacher, miracles, and healings, also mentions helps (1 Cor. 12:28). An army contains a lot more privates than it does generals. And while the generals are important as directors of the battle, most of the actual work of fighting the enemy is done by the privates. I personally feel that most of the soul winning should be done by church members and not by just the pastor.

You are created by God, and loved by God. If you are a Christian, you're the King's kid; He wants to use you. That's what counts.

Everyone of us can work for God. When we are kind and loving to our family, we are reflecting His love. And much more, when we show love to a stranger or an enemy, we show His love.

How can we do this? We may say, "I don't feel loving toward this or that person." Love is more than a comfortable emotion; love is a conscious decision. It's a commitment.

In the choir that my wife belongs to, they have what they call "Prayer Partners," something like secret pals. They keep the same partner for a month or two, and then reveal who they have been praying for and change for another month or two.

One month she had the one person in the choir that she had the hardest time liking. She said this person had never done anything to upset her, she just irritated her by existing. Barb was positive that God had to have a real sense of humor to see that she had to pray for this person. But she found that as she began to pray for this person, and to look for cards of encouragement to send to her, God really began to do a work in her own life. By the end of the two months, God had placed a real compassion in her heart. Barb says that she no longer has the negative reaction she did have. She actually feels love.

When we begin to act lovingly, the feelings of love soon follow. We can show God's love by reaching out to those around us. God loved and He gave. As we give, we show His love.

Maybe you think you have nothing to give. Anyone can give a kind word, or a few moments of patience. There are opportunities all around you, if you only look for them. Make a list of the kind things you do each week.

Your neighbor who has a sick child would appreciate a meal brought in, or perhaps an offer of help with her laundry.

Maybe a young couple really needs some time by themselves. Offer to take their children for a few hours.

You're a great handymen, but the man next door doesn't know which end of a screwdriver is which, and his house is beginning to look like it. Offer to drive a few well-placed nails, and maybe show him how to make those minor repairs. It helps your own property values when the neighborhood is kept up.

Do you know someone who is lonely? (I think we all do.) Be a friend. Make a phone call, invite someone to go to church with you. Invite someone to come over for dinner.

Do you have an elderly friend who lives alone? Assure him/her that you are concerned. A short phone call every day, that can be counted on, is a big relief.

A friend of ours who is quite elderly, but also quite independent, slipped in his bathtub. The fall frightened him, but most frightening was the thought that if he hadn't managed to get himself up, maybe no one would have missed him or thought to look for him until it was much too late.

Now, we have him call us every morning at a certain time just to let us know that he has finished his shower, and is all right. When we are out of town, someone else takes over.

If we don't hear from him by a certain time, we call him, and make sure he has just overslept. Yes, someday he will go to meet his Lord, and he may be alone when it happens, but the possibility of lying in his house for days helpless and alone and suffering no longer exists. This is ministry.

Look for ways to make your life a blessing. Learn to be creative in the ways you give and to make your giving a witness for the Lord. Your own lifestyle can be radical.

Is it time yet to rethink how we Christians do things?

The dictionary defines a principle as a basic truth, a rule, or concept. It also says that a method is a system, way, or process.

Our principles should never change: a faith in the atoning work of Christ on the cross, honesty, biblical holiness, and love for one another, among others. But our methods must keep peace with the times.

If we look back through the history of the Church we will find that many changes have taken place. The early Christians met in homes, often secretly. When Constantine embraced this new religion and legalized it, the era of building bigger and bigger churches began.

As Christianity became a state religion, any practice that was not officially sanctioned by the Pope became dangerous, and it was not until comparatively recent times that real religious freedom came on the scene.

Even the Puritans, who came to this country in 1620 seeking religious freedom, were not seeking it for everyone, only for themselves. Every generation seems to have those who feel that their method is the only correct one.

Throughout this entire time, true believers in Christ many times have had to alter their methods, in order not to compromise their principles. Over the years there were many reconsidered positions.

In the world around us, there have been many changes in technology in our lifetime. Many who are still living now can remember when horses and buggies were the standard means of transportation. Now we drive computerized automobiles.

Today most offices have at least one computer and a copier, instead of just a typewriter. Many offices also have a facsimile transmitter or a fax machine.

The field of medicine has also radically

changed. Antibiotics and vaccines have virtually eradicated some diseases.

We don't keep house or cook the same way we did even 15 years ago. The advent of frozen and freeze-dried foods, as well as pre-packaged dinners, has drastically changed our eating habits. We no longer do laundry on a washboard or scrub floors on our knees. We cross the continent in a matter of hours, not in months. Yes, there are some who feel that the methods of the Church should never change. They feel that if it has never been done this way before, why try it now. This, of course, can hold up the progress of winning souls, which is exactly what Satan wants.

It has been aptly said that the function of the local church is fourfold: worship, information, fellowship, and evangelism. The listing is not necessarily in order of importance.

Satan doesn't want any church to be successful in any of her functions, but especially not in the field of evangelism. Any method he can use to make this ineffectual will be used. These can include hampering the traditional revival, personal witnessing, Christian music, drama, children's evangelism, and any other method.

Satan is willing to adapt his methods. He will make the gospel seem unpalatable because the method of delivering it is too drab, or because it is too modern, depending on the taste of the person that he is working on. He is willing to keep experimenting until he finds just the right combination to discourage you.

To be in agreement with Satan is to be against God. To say something can't be done, you are in agreement with Satan.

We must learn that methods can be changed in order to keep up with the times.

The "Super Church" concept, which is somewhat of a cross between a high school pep rally and the "Mickey Mouse Club," has replaced the traditional Sunday school in some areas. This is neither good nor bad — the bottom line is how effective it is, how many children it reaches. Touching lives is what counts.

Many churches have replaced the standard mid-week prayer meeting and Bible study with home meetings. Both methods are equally correct, both can accomplish the same purpose. Each method is criticized by proponents of the other method.

Some churches have begun using newer translations of the Bible as their preferred version. Others feel that if the King James Version was "good enough for Paul and Silas, it's good enough for me."

Some churches use only hymnbooks as a source of songs, some use only choruses and an overhead projector. Others prefer to use both. Either can glorify God.

Christian music has also changed and broadened its range of styles. Just as fashion allows us to wear many different styles of clothing, so Christian lyrics can be set to music of any style, from classical to country to pop to "heavy metal" rock.

The use of radio as a medium for spreading the gospel was not readily accepted, nor was TV. Now some of the very folks who fought against them seem to feel that they don't need anything else, and rarely attend and support a local church. They are now for the very thing they were against. They stay home from church to watch their favorite Christian programs.

We personally have altered our methods many times during our years of ministry. We have traveled for most of our adult lives. We started out traveling in a car and later progressed to a motor coach, but now I fly commercially in order to get to my appearances. I let the band, *Illustrator*, beat the road in the coach and semi-truck.

Our methods of preaching the gospel have changed several times during those years. God gave me the vision of using music with our ministry. First, Barb and I sang as a duet, accompanying ourselves with a guitar and an accordion. Then, as the children came along and grew up, we added them to the music.

By the early seventies, our boys Nathan and Dan, and my brother Mike, formed a band, and Barb and I dropped out. Their contemporary style, using guitars and drums was a little too much for some churches, and even for us. Some even thought that their music was of the devil. (The term contemporary only means "belonging to this present time.")

However, their music has been used to bring thousands of young people to know the Lord. Now some of these same churches who didn't believe in this music have similar bands of their own.

We have a board and have accountability. We make changes as time goes on, to be the most effective. We are governed by management and decision. We are operating in the will of God and the fruit of our labor is evident.

The band, *Illustrator*, a youth arm of our ministry, has made some changes in order to do what God has called them to do. They constantly update their equipment in order to be more effective. They keep their musical style current, their testimony remains constant, but the message is almost 2,000 years old. "Jesus died for you because He loves you."

It doesn't hurt to keep an open mind where new methods are concerned. Maybe each of us needs to take stock and see if perhaps by altering some of our methods, without compromising our principles, we might be able to touch more lives with the gospel.

The apostle Paul expressed it well: "I am made all things to all men, that I might by all means save some" (1 Cor. 9:22).

11

What Can We Do When the Odds Are Against Us?

The writer of Hebrews states that first we must believe that God exists, and then that He rewards those who seek Him. God is our source, a rewarder; He is a positive God and a God of success and has a plan for your life. He loves you. He made only one of you, and you belong to Him. He responds to your faith.

Satan is a deceiver, a destroyer, a devourer, and a thief. All that Satan has is stolen goods, and he wants to hijack your life. He is negative. However, he also has a plan for your life that leads to destruction and ruin. He works through your fears. He will play mind games with you.

You need to understand that you are in a war. You can help tip the scales of the battle in your favor by obedience to the Word of God.

You can lose the battle by your disobedience, stubbornness, and unforgiving spirit. Deuteronomy 28 discusses this quite thoroughly. We often help create our own problems, but we can also overcome them with God's help.

Here are some ideas that will help you if you follow them diligently:

1. Begin every day with God (see Matt. 6:33).

The bottom line in your life should be to put God first, take Him as your partner, have a real honest bond between Him and you, and commit your life to Him.

Start each day with prayer. Continue with prayer throughout the day.

If you leave God out of the plan for your life, you can't expect answers. Give Him a chance to work His plan in your life. Don't do your thing, do God's.

2. Take inventory of your life.

You know where you have been, where you are now, and what basic goals you have. You know what has gone right and wrong. Write it all down on paper. Do it like a warehouse inventory.

3. Forgive those who have wronged you.

You will never be a success or be in God's perfect will without forgiving.

If you have mistreated someone, been dishonest, or lied, make it right. Then watch the odds that are against you turn around. It's hard to "eat crow," but it's worth it.

Don't justify your bad attitudes and unkind words. Be the one to restore the relationship. It doesn't matter who started it, or who is really at fault. Bitterness will destroy you, so be a forgiving person.

4. Recognize Satan and his tactics.

Satan wants to hijack your future. He doesn't want you to be a good steward of finances. He doesn't want you to pay tithes or attend church or pray or read the Bible or witness to others.

5. Don't panic and give up.

It will cause you to lose control and may also kill the miracle God has planned for you. Discouragement is a tool of Satan. He knows that you will be more likely to give up if he can make you panic.

6. Assassinate negativism and discouragement.

They are tools of Satan. Refuse to look at anything in a negative manner. Look on the bright side. Be a positive force in a negative world. Forgive all who have had a negative influence in your life.

7. Develop a good attitude.

Your attitude is more important than your

IQ. Life is 10 percent of what happens to you and 90 percent of how you react to situations.

8. Obey God's commandments.

Deuteronomy 28 is a chapter you should really take time to study. You will see how to qualify for God's best blessings.

9. Be a giver.

Every day, give something to someone. Buy a stranger a cup of coffee, give of your time, help someone. This alone will open many new doors for you.

10. Start praising God (in advance) for your miracle.

My granddaughter, Jannessa, and I were in a mall. She said, "Papa, can we get some ice cream?"

I answered, "No, Jannessa, we don't have time." A few minutes later, she tried again, but my answer was the same.

Finally, in desperation she said, "Papa, I just wanted to tell you that if we did have time, I want to thank you in advance for the ice cream." Then she looked up into my eyes, and said, "I love you very much, Papa." Needless to say, we found time for the ice cream. Her thanks and expression of love in advance opened my heart.

Jesus tells us that if we, as imperfect parents, know how to give good things to our children, our Heavenly Father surely knows how to give us good things when we ask.

Make a practice daily of these points and watch God help you.

Does God always know where you are?

Two friends of mine, who I will call John and Susan, had been having some problems in their marriage. I had counseled them many times, but the problems got worse.

One evening, I felt a strong urge to telephone them. After I had dialed their number, a strange, gruff sounding man answered. "Who is this?" he growled.

I told him my name. "I never heard of Ken Gaub," he retorted. Then he added, "Hey, Susan, do you know a Ken Gaub?"

In a moment, she had taken the receiver. "Yes," she told him. "Ken," she asked, "how did you get this number? I have left John. My new friend's phone is unlisted."

"Susan," I said, "I just dialed your home phone. I don't know how I reached this phone. You had better get out of there and go home as quick as you can!"

By now she was crying. "I will," she agreed.

We both hung up. I dialed the number again. John answered. "Ken," he began, "Susan is gone. We are in trouble."

I answered, "John, God is a God of miracles. I just talked to Susan, and she is on her way home."

We talked for a while about how to deal with the situation. I asked him to call me as soon as she returned. He did. Today their marriage is solid.

What are the odds of dialing a telephone

number and having it ring the unlisted telephone of a man you have never met, where an affair is about to take place?

God can turn your situation around. The odds may be against you, but remember, God is against the odds.

If you would like to get in touch with Ken Gaub you can reach him at:

Ken Gaub
World Wide Ministries
P.O. Box 1
Yakima, Washington 98907 U.S.A.
Phone: (509) 575-1965
FAX (509) 575-4732

Books by Ken Gaub

Dreams, Plans, Goals

Maybe you have a dream but you're afraid to verbalize it or even pray about it because it appears impossible. Let Ken Gaub show you how to plan for the future and set goals that will make your dreams happen.

Discover practical ways to turn your dreams into reality, make your plans succeed, set goals, and achieve them.   *$7.95*

God's Got Your Number

Do you wonder if miracles from God truly occur in today's world? Are you afraid walking in Christian faith requires too much sacrifice? Then perhaps you've never received a phone call from heaven.

Ken Gaub did, and for this world evangelist it was a wake-up call that the God who talked with Adam in the cool of the Garden has never abandoned mankind, and stays in close contact with us still today.   *$7.95*

Answers to Questions You've Always Wanted to Ask

It has been said that the only dumb question is the one you don't ask when you're looking for an answer. Ken Gaub uses this book to ask and answer questions many Christians ask themselves every day. He combines the wit of a stand-up comic with insight gained from years in the ministry.

Gaub gives helpful tips on "loving the unloved," healing church rifts, and much more. Chances are, not only will you find the answer to a question you have, but many practical lessons will be absorbed from reading this timely book.   *$7.95*

**Available at Christian bookstores nationwide
or call 1-800-643-9535**